THE EU PRIVATE DAMAGES DIRECTIVE – PRACTICAL INSIGHTS

THE EU PRIVATE DAMAGES DIRECTIVE – PRACTICAL INSIGHTS

Minutes of the Closed Workshop 2015

Frank Wijckmans
Maaike Visser
Sarah Jaques
Evi Noël

intersentia
Cambridge – Antwerp – Portland

Intersentia Ltd
Sheraton House | Castle Park
Cambridge | CB3 0AX | United Kingdom
Tel.: +44 1223 370 170 | Fax: +44 1223 370 169
Email: mail@intersentia.co.uk
www.intersentia.com | www.intersentia.co.uk

Distribution for the UK and Ireland:
NBN International
Airport Business Centre, 10 Thornbury Road
Plymouth, PL6 7 PP
United Kingdom
Tel.: +44 1752 202 301 | Fax: +44 1752 202 331
Email: orders@nbninternational.com

Distribution for Europe and all other countries:
Intersentia Publishing nv
Groenstraat 31
2640 Mortsel
Belgium
Tel.: +32 3 680 15 50 | Fax: +32 3 658 71 21
Email: mail@intersentia.be

Distribution for the USA and Canada:
International Specialized Book Services
920 NE 58th Ave. Suite 300
Portland, OR 97213
USA
Tel.: +1 800 944 6190 (toll free) | Fax: +1 503 280 8832
Email: info@isbs.com

The EU Private Damages Directive – Practical Insights. Minutes of the Closed Workshop 2015

ISBN 978-1-78068-382-9
D/2016/7849/58
NUR 827

British Library Cataloguing in Publication Data. A catalogue record for this book is available from the British Library.

CONTENTS

LIST OF ABBREVIATIONS

Brussels I Regulation	Council Regulation (EC) No 44/2001 of 22 December 2000 on jurisdiction and the recognition and enforcement of judgments in civil and commercial matters [2001] OJ L12/1
Brussels I bis Regulation	Regulation (EU) No 1215/2012 of 12 December 2012 of the European Parliament and of the Council on jurisdiction and the recognition and enforcement of judgments in civil and commercial matters [2012] OJ L351/1
Commission	European Commission
Court of Justice	Court of Justice of the European Union
EEA	European Economic Area
EU	European Union
EU Courts	General Court and Court of Justice
Horizontal Guidelines	Guidelines on the applicability of Article 101 of the Treaty on the Functioning of the European Union to horizontal cooperation agreements [2011] OJ C11/1
Leniency Notice	Commission Notice on immunity from fines and reduction of fines in cartel cases [2006] OJ C298/17
NCA/NCAs	National Competition Authority/Authorities
PDD	Directive (EU) No 104/2014 of 26 November 2014 of the European Parliament and of the Council on certain rules governing actions for damages under national law for infringements of the competition law provisions of the Member States and of the European Union [2014] OJ L349/1

Quantifying Harm Communication	Communication from the Commission on quantifying harm in actions for damages based on breaches of Article 101 or 102 of the Treaty on the Functioning of the European Union [2013] OJ C167/19, http://eur-lex.europa.eu/LexUriServ/LexUriServ.do?uri=OJ:C:2013:167:0019:0021:EN:PDF
Quantifying Harm Practical Guide	Practical Guide quantifying harm in actions for damages based on breaches of Article 101 or 102 of the Treaty on the Functioning of the European Union, SWD(2013) 205, 11.06.2013, http://ec.europa.eu/competition/antitrust/actionsdamages/quantification_guide_en.pdf
R&D	Research and Development
Regulation 1206/2001	Council Regulation (EC) No 1206/2001 of 28 May 2001 on cooperation between the courts of the Member States in the taking of evidence in civil or commercial matters [2001] OJ L174/1
Regulation 1/2003	Council Regulation (EC) No 1/2003 of 16 December 2002 on the implementation of the rules on competition laid down in Articles 81 and 82 of the Treaty [2003] OJ L1/1
Regulation 139/2004	Council Regulation (EC) No 139/2004 of 20 January 2004 on the control of concentrations between undertakings [2004] OJ L24/1
Settlement Notice	Commission Notice on the conduct of settlement procedures in view of the adoption of Decisions pursuant to Article 7 and Article 23 of Council Regulation (EC) No 1/2003 in cartel cases [2008] OJ C167/1
SME/SMEs	Small and Medium-sized Enterprise/Enterprises
TFEU	Treaty on the Functioning of the European Union [2010] OJ C83/47

INTRODUCTION

These are the Minutes of a Closed Workshop organised on 21 May 2015 in Brussels, Belgium. The Closed Workshop was entirely dedicated to the PDD.[1]

The Closed Workshop was attended by a group of competition law specialists covering the majority of the Member States. A complete list of the attendees is included in Annex 2 to the Minutes.

The exchange of views during the Closed Workshop was structured as follows. For each Chapter of the PDD a brief introduction was provided. This was then followed by an in-depth discussion of selected issues of interpretation gathered from the participating practitioners.

The Minutes adhere to the same structure so that each section of the Minutes corresponds to a chapter of the PDD. Every section commences with a description of the general context within which the specific questions addressed during the Closed Workshop must be placed and understood. The outcome of the actual discussion of the specific questions is then provided in a Q&A format, very much resembling the approach used in the Closed Workshop.

Given the format of the Closed Workshop, inevitably only selected interpretation issues came up and are addressed in these Minutes. The Minutes therefore do not aim to provide a complete commentary or interpretation guide on the PDD. Furthermore, the Minutes reflect the outcome of a debate and are therefore not intended as legal advice, nor as a reflection of the position of the individual law firms involved or of the Commission on the matters addressed.

By the same token, given the depth of the discussions that took place during the Closed Workshop we are convinced that the Minutes provide useful and meaningful guidance. The joint effort during the Closed Workshop has resulted in a level of understanding of certain aspects of the PDD that to our knowledge have so far not been published.

---

1 Directive (EU) No 104/2014 of 26 November 2014 of the European Parliament and of the Council on certain rules governing actions for damages under national law for infringements of the competition law provisions of the Member States and of the European Union [2014] OJ L349/1.

We are grateful to Filip Tuytschaever for reviewing an earlier version of these Minutes.

We like to thank Eddy De Smijter (DG Competition, Head of Unit, ECN and Private Enforcement), Martin Seegers (Cartel Damage Claims), Ben Bornemann (Cartel Damage Claims) and Anneli Howard (Monckton Chambers) for having shared their personal experience with the issue of private damages actions during the Closed Workshop.

Finally, we would like to express our gratitude to the participants in the Closed Workshop. In addition to being very sound practitioners, they were simply an interesting and pleasant group to undertake this PDD journey with.

***

Frank Wijckmans is partner of **contrast**, European & Business Law. He is specialized in EU and national competition law. He is Professor at the Brussels School of Competition and has an extensive publication record within his field of expertise. Frank Wijckmans chaired the Closed Workshop.

Maaike Visser is counsel within the EU & competition team of **contrast**, European & Business Law.

Sarah Jaques is associate within the EU & competition team of **contrast**, European & Business Law.

Evi Noël is paralegal within the EU & competition team of **contrast**, European & Business Law.

CHAPTER I

SUBJECT-MATTER, SCOPE AND DEFINITIONS

1. GENERAL CONTEXT

1. **Chapter I PDD** contains provisions on the subject-matter, scope and definitions used in the PDD (Articles 1–4 PDD).

2. The subject-matter of the PDD is the private enforcement of Articles 101 and 102 TFEU.[2] Articles 101 and 102 TFEU produce direct effects in relationships between individuals and create, for the individuals concerned, rights and obligations which can be enforced before the national courts (private enforcement).[3]

3. Private enforcement must be distinguished from public enforcement. Public enforcement is regulated by Regulation 1/2003,[4] which contains provisions governing the powers of enforcement of the Commission, the NCAs[5] and the EU Courts in relation to Articles 101 and 102 TFEU. It is acknowledged in the case law of the EU Courts that private and public enforcement interact with each other and that private enforcement "strengthens the working of the Community competition rules by deterring anticompetitive conduct as well as fully compensating those who have suffered harm as a result of the conduct".[6]

---

2 Treaty on the Functioning of the European Union [2010] OJ C83/47.

3 Case C-282/95 P, 18 March 1997, ECLI:EU:C:1997:159, *Guérin automobiles/Commission*, para 39 and Case 127/73, 27 March 1974, ECLI:EU:C:1974:25, *BRT*, para 16.

4 Council Regulation (EC) No 1/2003 of 16 December 2002 on the implementation of the rules on competition laid down in Articles 81 and 82 of the Treaty [2003] OJ L1/1.

5 For the purpose of this text and in accordance with Article 2(7) PDD, an NCA means "an authority designated by a Member State pursuant to Article 35 of Regulation (EC) No 1/2003, as being responsible for the application of Articles 101 and 102 TFEU". When using the term "competition authority", however, this text refers to the Commission or an NCA or both, as the context may require.

6 Case C-557/12, 5 June 2014, ECLI:EU:C:2014:1317, *Kone and Others*, para 23; Case C-536/11, 6 June 2013, ECLI:EU:C:2013:366, *Donau Chemie and Others*, paras 23–24 and Case C-453/99, 20 September 2001, ECLI:EU:C:2001:465, *Courage*, paras 26–27.

4. Prior to the adoption of the PDD, it was felt that private enforcement was underdeveloped and that private proceedings were uncertain and ineffective in the EU.[7] The PDD therefore seeks to ensure "a more level playing field for undertakings operating in the internal market and to improve the conditions for consumers to exercise the rights they derive from the internal market (...) and to reduce the differences between the Member States as to the national rules governing actions for damages for [competition law infringements]" (recital 9 PDD).

5. The subject-matter and scope of the PDD are addressed in Article 1 PDD. Article 1(1) PDD is the central provision. The provision relies on certain defined terms and familiar competition law concepts. This triggers the immediate question whether these concepts must, for the purposes of private enforcement under the PDD, be given the same meaning as in the public enforcement of competition law.

6. Article 2 PDD contains an extensive list of 24 definitions, which clarify the scope of the key concepts in the PDD. It is important to systematically refer back to these definitions as they provide often substantive input that is essential to the correct application and interpretation of the substantive provisions of the PDD. The Closed Workshop focused on the definitions appearing in multiple provisions in the PDD.

7. "Infringement of competition law" is clearly one of the key concepts of the PDD. The concept is defined in Article 2(1) PDD and reference is made to it in many other definitions including the definition of "infringer" (Article 2(2) PDD), "claim for damages" (Article 2(5) PDD), "injured party" (Article 2(6) PDD) and "infringement decision" (Article 2(11) PDD). Another important element in the definition of "infringement of competition law" is the explicit reference to "national competition law". "National competition law" is defined in the PDD by reference to Article 3(1) Regulation 1/2003.

8. The definition of "action for damages", found in Article 2(4) PDD, obviously plays a central role. It serves to circumscribe the national actions to which the provisions of the PDD apply. The defined notion of "action for damages" is relied upon in the following provisions of the PDD: the disclosure of evidence (Articles 5–8 PDD); the effect of national decisions (Article 9 PDD); the passing-on defence (Article 13 PDD); indirect purchaser (Article 14

---

7 Green Paper, *Damages actions for breach of the EC antitrust* rules, COM(2005) 672, 19.12.2005 and accompanying Commission Staff Working Paper, SEC(2005) 1732, 19.12.2005, 15–17 and A. Howard, "Too little, too late? The European Commission's Legislative Proposals on Anti-Trust Damages Actions", *Journal of European Competition Law & Practice* 2013, 456.

PDD); actions for damages by claimants from different levels in the supply chain (Article 15 PDD); and suspensive and other effects of consensual dispute resolution (Article 18 PDD).

9. The Closed Workshop furthermore addressed the concept of a "cartel". This concept is defined in Article 2(14) PDD. While the scope of the PDD is not confined to cartel infringements, such infringements stand out as they attract a rebuttable presumption of having caused harm (Article 17(2) PDD).

10. Given the importance of the interplay between the PDD and leniency, quite a number of definitions are dedicated to various aspects of the leniency regime: the "leniency programme" (Article 2(15) PDD); the "leniency statement" (Article 2(16) PDD); and the "immunity recipient" (Article 2(19) PDD). The Closed Workshop focused on the definitions of "leniency statement" and "immunity recipient".

11. Another important concept in the PDD is the right to compensation, which is addressed in Article 3 PDD. The right to compensation is not new in EU law. It has been developed in the case law of the EU Courts[8] and is an established principle that is equally applicable to infringements of Articles 101 and 102 TFEU.[9]

12. There are two important concepts that govern the right to compensation of an injured party: (i) the right to full compensation and (ii) the prohibition of overcompensation.

13. Article 3(1) PDD refers to the fact that harm caused by an infringement of competition law should be fully compensated. Full compensation must ensure that a person who has suffered harm is placed in the position which that person would have been in had the infringement of competition law not been committed (Article 3(2) PDD).

14. In order to claim compensation, a claimant must show that there is a causal relationship between the harm suffered and an infringement of competition law.[10]

15. The PDD excludes the possibility of overcompensation, whether by means of punitive, multiple or other types of damages (Article 3(3) PDD). In most

---

8 See Case C-213/89, 19 June 1990, ECLI:EU:C:1990:257, *Factortame*, para 19 and Case 106/77, 9 March 1978, ECLI:EU:C:1978:49, *Simmenthal*, para 16.

9 Joined Cases C-295/04 to C-298/04, 13 July 2006, ECLI:EU:C:2006:461, *Manfredi*, para 89 and Case C-453/99, 20 September 2001, ECLI:EU:C:2001:465, *Courage*, para 25.

10 Recital 11 PDD refers to the case law of the Court of Justice in *Manfredi*, see Joined Cases C-295/04 to C-298/04, 13 July 2006, ECLI:EU:C:2006:461, *Manfredi*, para 61.

Member States, damages are essentially compensatory and intend to provide reparation for both economic and non-economic losses. Punitive damages serve clearly different purposes, namely to punish the offender, to deter the offender and other potential offenders, to reward the plaintiff for enforcing the law and/or to supplement inadequate compensatory damages. Commissioner Almunia confirmed that private enforcement in the EU is about compensation and that "sanctioning EU competition law infringements is and should remain the exclusive task of competition authorities".[11]

16. By including the prohibition to overcompensate in the PDD, the Commission clearly intends to distinguish damages actions in the EU from damages actions in the US, where punitive damages are available. On the basis of the Clayton Act[12] US courts automatically treble the damages for US private litigants.[13]

17. Reference to the general principles of effectiveness and equivalence of EU law is made in Article 4 PDD. These general principles require Member States, in the absence of EU law, to ensure that national procedural law allows for the effective exercise of an individual's right to compensation.[14]

18. Actions before national courts, which seek to enforce a right derived from EU law, are governed by national rules and national procedures. The EU principle of effectiveness requires Member States to ensure that such national rules and procedures are not applied in a way that makes it excessively difficult or practically impossible to exercise the right to compensation. The EU principle of equivalence requires national rules and procedures to be no less favourable than those applying to actions seeking to enforce a similar right granted under national law (recital 11 PDD).[15]

19. The EU principle of equivalence is reflected in Article 4 PDD and applies to all national rules governing the exercise of the right to compensation for harm resulting from an infringement of Article 101 or Article 102 TFEU. The

---

11 J. Almunia, *Antitrust Damages in EU Law and Policy*, SPEECH/13/887, http://europa.eu/rapid/press-release_SPEECH-13-887_en.htm.

12 Clayton Act (US) 15 October 1914, codified at 15 U.S.C. §12–27.

13 Section 4 Clayton Act states that "any person who shall be injured in his business or property by reason of anything forbidden in the antitrust laws (...) shall recover threefold the damages by him sustained, and the cost of suit, including a reasonable attorney's fee". See also B. Scharaw, "Commission proposal for a Directive on antitrust damages and recommendation on principles for collective redress – the road towards 'Private Antitrust Enforcement' in the European Union?", *ECLR* 2014, 355.

14 Joined Cases C-295/04 to C-298/04, 13 July 2006, ECLI:EU:C:2006:461, *Manfredi*, paras 62, 72 and 81.

15 Case 33/76, 16 December 1976, ECLI:EU:C:1976:188, *Rewe*, para 5.

principle applies likewise to national rules on aspects not expressly dealt with in the PDD, such as the causal relationship between the infringement and the harm (recital 11 PDD).

20. **Recitals 1–13 PDD** can usefully be consulted for the purposes of clarifying the matters addressed in Chapter 1 PDD (notably subject-matter, scope, right to compensation and the principles of effectiveness and equivalence contained in the PDD).

2. DISCUSSION OF RELEVANT PROVISIONS OF THE PDD

A. ARTICLE 1 PDD: SUBJECT-MATTER AND SCOPE

1. This Directive sets out certain rules necessary to ensure that anyone who has suffered harm caused by an infringement of competition law by an undertaking or by an association of undertakings, can effectively exercise the right to claim full compensation for that harm from that undertaking or association.

2. This Directive sets out rules coordinating the enforcement of the competition rules by competition authorities and the enforcement of those rules in damages actions before national courts.

Question:

21. Article 1(1) PDD refers to "an infringement of competition law". What does "competition law" encompass in the definition of "an infringement of competition law"? What types of practices are covered by the PDD? Is it only limited to practices falling under Articles 101 and 102 TFEU or does it also cover state aid and merger control?

Answer:

22. Article 1(1) PDD refers to "an infringement of competition law". Article 2(1) PDD defines "an infringement of competition law" as "an infringement of Article 101 or 102 TFEU, or of national competition law". The PDD therefore intends to cover antitrust in all its aspects and surely not only cartels. Infringements related to distribution and licensing relationships, soft horizontals, such as joint R&D or specialisation, information exchanges and the like are likewise covered. Any practice that is caught by either Article 101 or Article 102 TFEU can therefore lead to a private damages claim governed by the PDD.

23. The reference in the definition to Articles 101 and 102 TFEU excludes by definition anti-competitive practices in the sphere of state aid. State aid is governed by Article 107 TFEU and following. The definition contained in Article 2(1) PDD also implies that merger control is not covered to the extent that it is governed by Regulation 139/2004.[16]

24. Article 106 TFEU contains a prohibition on Member States adopting or maintaining in force measures relating to public undertakings or undertakings entrusted with special or exclusive rights contrary to the TFEU. Article 106 TFEU must be applied together with, *inter alia*, Articles 101 and 102 TFEU. Recital 3 PDD confirms that the right to compensation in EU law equally applies to infringements of Articles 101 and 102 TFEU by public undertakings and by undertakings entrusted with special or exclusive rights. The scope of the PDD therefore also covers all situations where Articles 101 and/or 102 TFEU are applied in combination with Article 106 TFEU.

Question:

25. The concepts of "undertaking" and "association of undertakings" are very familiar in competition law and have been further developed in the case law of the EU Courts. Can the competition law concepts of "undertaking" and "association of undertakings" be transposed to damages proceedings before the national courts or must they be given an autonomous interpretation in the context of the PDD?

Answer:

26. Article 1(1) PDD refers to an "undertaking" and an "association of undertakings". These two concepts are also contained in Articles 101 and 102 TFEU. They are not neutral concepts and have indeed been developed in the case law of the EU Courts.[17] The text in the PDD links the concept of infringement by an undertaking/association of undertakings to the civil liability of that same undertaking/association of undertakings. It may therefore seem logical that the interpretation of both concepts is the same in the context of Articles 101 and 102 TFEU, as well as in cases of civil liability pursued in accordance with the PDD.

---

16 Council Regulation (EC) No 139/2004 of 20 January 2004 on the control of concentrations between undertakings [2004] OJ L24/1.

17 For the concept of "undertaking", see Case C-440/11 P, 11 July 2013, ECLI:EU:C:2013:514, *Commission/Stichting Administratiekantoor Portielje and Gosselin Group*, para 36; Case C-309/99, 19 February 2002, ECLI:EU:C:2002:98, *Wouters and Others*, para 46; and Case C-41/90, 23 April 1991, ECLI:EU:C:1991:161, *Klaus Höfner and Fritz Elser*, para 21. For the concept of "association of undertaking", see Opinion Advocate General Léger in Case C-309/99, 10 July 2001, ECLI:EU:C:2001:390, *Wouters and Others*, para 61.

27. Until now, civil liability has been a domain of national law which, with limited exceptions, was left untouched by EU law. Against this background, it needs to be confirmed whether all aspects of the concepts of "undertaking" and "association of undertakings" that can be found in the public enforcement of competition law automatically apply to the PDD. Future case law will need to clarify this.

28. In most jurisdictions, national law links civil liability to faults committed by specific legal entities. By referring to "undertaking" the PDD may have enlarged the scope of civil liability on account of competition law infringements. According to the case law of the EU Courts, the concept of undertaking can be wider than a single legal entity and may also encompass group companies.[18] As such, the reference to "undertaking" triggers questions as to whether the PDD covers claims addressed to group companies (e.g. the parent company) that are not directly involved in the infringement. This issue is not resolved in the PDD and it will be for the EU Courts to interpret the concept of undertaking in the PDD and to resolve this question. This is most likely one of the most compelling questions that remains to be addressed with regard to these concepts.

29. The relevance of this issue is not merely theoretical. In cases where groups are involved that have locations outside the EEA (which may trigger jurisdictional and other private international law issues) or where the companies directly involved in the infringement lack the resources to pay the required compensation or have undergone restructuring, the broader concept used in the public enforcement of EU competition law may be of direct relevance for facilitating or even bringing a civil damages claim.

Question:

30. The "economic succession" theory is relied upon in a situation where an entity that committed a competition law infringement ceased to exist. On the basis of that theory, which has been developed by the EU Courts,[19] the legal entity that acquired the relevant business that was involved in the infringement

---

[18] Case C-501/11 P, 18 July 2013, ECLI:EU:C:2013:522, *Schindler Holding and Others/Commission*, para 112; Joined Cases C-628/10 P and C-14/11 P, 19 July 2012, ECLI:EU:C:2012:479, *Alliance One International and Standard Commercial Tobacco/Commission and Commission/ Alliance One International and Others*, para 101; and Case C-97/08 P, 10 September 2009, ECLI:EU:C:2009:536, *Akzo Nobel and Others/Commission*, para 60.

[19] Case C-280/06, 11 December 2007, ECLI:EU:C:2007:775, *ETI and Others*; Joined Cases C-204/00 P and Others, 7 January 2004, ECLI:EU:C:2004:6, *Aalborg Portland and Others/ Commission*; Case C-49/92 P, 8 July 1999, ECLI:EU:C:1999:356, *Commission/Anic Partecipazioni* and Joined Cases 40/73 and Others, 16 December 1975, ECLI:EU:C:1975:174, *Suiker Unie and Others/Commission*.

will be held liable.[20] The successor is therefore held liable for the anti-competitive conduct of another legal person.[21] Is this theory also relevant for the civil liability under the PDD on the part of successors of the infringing undertakings that are no longer in existence?

Answer:

31. The text of the PDD clearly makes a link between an undertaking being held liable for an infringement of competition law and having to bear civil liability for such infringement. The PDD does not provide to what extent this link can be stretched, for instance on the basis of the theory of economic succession. It will be for the EU Courts to determine the exact implications of Article 1(1) PDD. The text of the PDD therefore does not exclude the possibility that the EU Courts may want to distinguish between liability for fines and civil liability and to avoid completely identical treatment of the personal scope in the two areas. It could also be that it wishes to bridge the concepts.

32. Currently, the PDD does not necessarily encompass the notion of economic succession. This point was left open. In order to have this interpretation issue resolved, a preliminary ruling of the Court of Justice will most likely be needed.[22]

Question:

33. According to Article 23(4) Regulation 1/2003, members of an association of undertakings can be held liable for the fine imposed by the Commission or an NCA on an association of undertakings. Can a claim for civil damages under the PDD likewise be raised against the members of an association of undertakings?

---

20 See A. Brown and M. Schonberg, "Widening the Net: The General Court Extends the Principle of Successor Liability in EU Competition Law", *ECLR* 2013, 34 and F. Wijckmans, "Attribution of cartel liability" in F. Wijckmans and F. Tuytschaever (eds.), *Horizontal Agreements and Cartels in EU Competition Law*, Oxford, Oxford University Press, 2015, 235–266.

21 Case C-297/98 P, 16 November 2000, ECLI:EU:C:2000:633, *SCA Holding/Commission*, para 29.

22 There is already Finnish national case law on the application of the principle of economic succession to private damages cases. See H. Laurila and T. Kalliokoski, "Developments in Finnish Private Antitrust Litigation: Finland Fast-Forwards into the Future?", *ECLR* 2014, 519–524. The Finnish District Court held that the doctrine of economic succession is a general principle of EU competition law, which is applicable to both public and private enforcement. It therefore applied the economic succession doctrine to antitrust damages.

Answer:

34. The aim of the PDD is to achieve full compensation for the harm caused by an infringement. The EU Courts may be expected not to accept easily legal scenarios avoiding full compensation for the victims. This does not necessarily mean that the members of an association will automatically be held liable. Contrary to Regulation 1/2003, it was not felt necessary to have a detailed provision in the PDD on the payment of damages. It might be that under existing national civil law only the association, as the infringer, may be held liable. This may change as the civil liability of associations of undertakings has now become an EU law concept and not purely a national civil law concept due to its explicit inclusion in the PDD. It may therefore receive an autonomous interpretation of the EU Courts that may diverge from the current thinking under national law.

35. Until such time as the EU Courts have resolved the issue, diverging approaches by the national courts cannot be excluded. Whether and under what conditions a civil claim can be lodged against both the association and its members is therefore not definitively resolved in the PDD.

B. ARTICLE 2(1) PDD: INFRINGEMENT OF COMPETITION LAW

> *"infringement of competition law" means an infringement of Article 101 or 102 TFEU, or of national competition law*

Question:

36. The definition of "infringement of competition law" refers to infringements of Article 101 or 102 TFEU or of national competition law. What is the meaning of the second "or" between "Article 101 or 102 TFEU" *or* "national competition law"? Does it mean that an infringement of competition law within meaning of the PDD can relate to an infringement of national competition law, without also being an infringement of Article 101 TFEU or Article 102 TFEU?

Answer:

37. This wording was discussed quite extensively during the preparation of the PDD. According to lawyer-linguists, the meaning of "or" can be "and", but the meaning of "and" can never be "or". This means that the PDD applies to infringements of Article 101 or 102 TFEU (clearly in the alternative). Such infringement can also be an infringement of national competition law, but must

not necessarily also be an infringement of national competition law in order to attract the application of the PDD.

38. In order to fully appreciate the reference to "or of national competition law" in Article 2(1) PDD, the definition of national competition law in Article 2(3) PDD must be taken into account. It is defined as "provisions of national law that predominantly pursue the same objective as Articles 101 and 102 TFEU and *that are applied to the same case and in parallel to Union competition law pursuant to Article 3(1) of Regulation (EC) No 1/2003* (...)".

39. According to Article 3(1) Regulation 1/2003[23] national competition law must be applied in conjunction with Article 101 or 102 TFEU where the "effect on trade" condition is met. The reference to "or of national competition law" in Article 2(1) PDD therefore refers to infringements sanctioned by national competition law in conjunction with Article 101 or 102 TFEU.

40. In short, the PDD applies to infringements of Article 101 *or* Article 102 TFEU (irrespective of whether such infringements also amount to an infringement of national competition law) and cases where national competition law is applied in conjunction with Article 101 or Article 102 TFEU. What is clearly not intended by the use of the word "or" is that the PDD applies to infringements of national competition law in cases where Article 101 or Article 102 TFEU do not also apply.[24]

C. ARTICLE 2(3) PDD: NATIONAL COMPETITION LAW

> *"national competition law" means provisions of national law that predominantly pursue the same objective as Articles 101 and 102 TFEU and that are applied to the same case and in parallel to Union competition law pursuant to Article 3(1) of Regulation (EC) No 1/2003, excluding provisions of national law which impose criminal penalties on natural persons, except to the extent that such criminal penalties are the means whereby competition rules applying to undertakings are enforced*

---

23 Article 3(1) Regulation 1/2003 provides that "where the competition authorities of the Member States or national courts apply national competition law to agreements, decisions by associations of undertakings or concerted practices within the meaning of Article [101(1) TFEU] which may affect trade between Member States within the meaning of that provision, they shall also apply Article [101 TFEU] to such agreements, decisions or concerted practices. Where the competition authorities of the Member States or national courts apply national competition law to any abuse prohibited by Article [102 TFEU], they shall also apply Article [102 TFEU]".

24 See final sentence recital 10 PDD: "This Directive should not affect actions for damages in respect of infringements of national competition law which do not affect trade between Member States within the meaning of Article 101 or 102 TFEU".

Question:

41. National competition law in the PDD is defined by reference to Article 3(1) Regulation 1/2003. In addition, certain provisions of national criminal law are excluded from the scope of the PDD. However, provisions of national criminal law that are "the means whereby competition rules applying to undertakings are enforced" are not excluded. Which provisions of national criminal law are specifically excluded from the definition of national competition law in the PDD, and which provisions should be considered "the means whereby competition rules applying to undertakings are enforced"?

Answer:

42. Recital 10 PDD confirms the extension of the scope of the PDD to actions for damages based on an infringement of national competition law where national competition law is applied pursuant to Article 3(1) Regulation 1/2003 (see above, para 39). Applying different rules on civil liability in respect of Article 101 or Article 102 TFEU and in respect of national competition law, even though they are applied in the same case in parallel, adversely affects the position of claimants. Such a hybrid approach would constitute an obstacle to the proper functioning of the internal market. The scope of "national competition law" in the PDD has therefore been made identical to the same concept that is used in Regulation 1/2003, notably those cases in which national competition law is applied in conjunction with Articles 101 and 102 TFEU.

43. In order to appreciate which provisions of national criminal law are excluded from the definition of national competition law in the PDD, reference must be made to recital 8 Regulation 1/2003.[25] Recital 8 Regulation 1/2003 contains exactly the same language as Article 2(3) PDD. It excludes provisions imposing criminal sanctions on natural persons, except to the extent that such sanctions are the means whereby competition rules applying to undertakings are enforced. Regulation 1/2003 was adopted at a time when a lively debate on the criminalisation of competition law was taking place. It was felt that criminalisation should not enter the scope of Regulation 1/2003 and should remain part of national criminal law. Hence, the basic principle is that national law imposing criminal sanctions on natural persons is not part of national competition law for the purposes of Regulation 1/2003 and therefore also not for the purposes of the PDD.

44. The exception to the exclusion of criminal law (which is contained both in recital 8 Regulation 1/2003 and Article 2(3) PDD) had to be included because of

25 See final sentence recital 8 Regulation 1/2003.

German competition law. The procedural rules that apply according to the German Act against Restraints of Competition[26] are included in the Act on Regulatory Offences[27], which is closely linked to German criminal procedural law. According to these (criminal) procedural rules, an undertaking can only be held liable for an infringement through an individual acting on behalf of the undertaking.[28] Such individuals are considered to be the actual infringers of competition law, and the undertaking is only liable as an indirect infringer ("*Nebenbetroffener*"), even when it receives the majority of the fines.[29] Recital 8 was therefore included in Regulation 1/2003 to avoid German competition law falling outside the scope of the Regulation as a result of the exclusion of criminal law. Given that the liability of undertakings can only be established through the establishment of an infringement by a natural person on the basis of criminal procedural laws, there was a perceived risk that, without this exclusion, German competition law would stay out of the reach of Regulation 1/2003 and now also the PDD.

D. ARTICLE 2(4) PDD: ACTION FOR DAMAGES

> *"action for damages" means an action under national law by which a claim for damages is brought before a national court by an alleged injured party, or by someone acting on behalf of one or more alleged injured parties where Union or national law provides for that possibility, or by a natural or legal person that succeeded in the right of the alleged injured party, including the person that acquired the claim*

26 Gesetz gegen Wettbewerbsbeschränkungen [Act Against Restraints of Competition] (DE) in the version published on 15 July 2005, Bundesgesetzblatt [Federal Law Gazette] I, page 2114; 2009 I, page 3850.

27 Gesetz über Ordnungswidrigkeiten [Act on Regulatory Offences] (DE) in the version published on 19 February 1987, Bundesgesetzblatt [Federal Law Gazette] I, page 602.

28 Section 30(1) Act on Regulatory Offences: "Where someone acting (1) as an entity authorised to represent a legal person or as a member of such an entity; (2) as chairman of the executive committee of an association without legal capacity or as a member of such committee; (3) as a partner authorised to represent a partnership with legal capacity, or (4) as the authorised representative with full power of attorney or in a managerial position as procura-holder or the authorised representative with a commercial power of attorney of a legal person or of an association of persons referred to in numbers 2 or 3; (5) as another person responsible on behalf of the management of the operation or enterprise forming part of a legal person, or of an association of persons referred to in numbers 2 or 3, also covering supervision of the conduct of business or other exercise of controlling powers in a managerial position; has committed a criminal offence or a regulatory offence as a result of which duties incumbent on the legal person or on the association of persons have been violated, or where the legal person or the association of persons has been enriched or was intended to be enriched, *a regulatory fine may be imposed on such person or association*" (emphasis added).

29 The maximum fine that can be imposed on natural persons is set at EUR 1 million; whereas the maximum level of the fine that can be imposed on undertakings is 10% of their global annual group turnover (see section 84(4) German Act against Restraints of Competition).

Question:

45. The definition of "action for damages" refers to "an action under national law" and "brought before a national court". "National law" and "national court" are two important concepts in order to appreciate which actions are included in the definition of "action for damages". What is the meaning of these concepts?

Answer:

46. The reference to "an action under national law" in the PDD must be understood as all actions for damages that exist under national law in the broadest sense. Actions under EU law that exist now or could exist in the future are therefore not automatically covered by the PDD.

47. A "national court" is defined in Article 2(9) PDD as "a court or tribunal of a Member State within the meaning of Article 267 TFEU". The notion of "court or tribunal" has been interpreted by the EU Courts.[30] In order to determine whether a body is a court or tribunal in the sense of EU law, a number of factors must be taken into account, such as whether the body is established by law, whether it is permanent, whether its jurisdiction is compulsory, whether its procedure is *inter partes*, whether it applies rules of law, and whether it is independent.[31] On the basis of the current case law, arbitral tribunals do not meet these conditions and are not considered a court or tribunal in the sense of Article 267 TFEU. Arbitral tribunals are therefore not covered by the PDD.

48. Hence, unless the national legislation implementing the PDD explicitly provides otherwise, the principles and procedures set forth in the PDD will not automatically govern arbitration proceedings in which a damage claim is brought on the basis of an infringement of the competition rules.

Question:

49. Recitals 3 and 13 PDD state that "anyone, be they an individual, including consumers, undertakings or a public authority" can be possible claimants of damages. When is there a sufficient interest according to the PDD to bring an action for damages?

---

[30] Case C-54/96, 17 September 1997, ECLI:EU:C:1997:413, *Dorsch Consult Ingenieursgesellschaft*, para 23.

[31] Case C-126/97, 1 June 1999, ECLI:EU:C:1999:269, *Eco Swiss China Time*, para 34 and Case 102/81, 23 March 1982, ECLI:EU:C:1982:107, *Nordsee Deutsche Hochseefischerei*, paras 10–12.

Answer:

50. The definition of an "action for damages" covers three different scenarios.

51. Firstly, an action can be brought by "an alleged injured party". The PDD defines an "injured party" in Article 2(6) PDD as "a person that has suffered harm caused by an infringement of competition law". The reference to an "alleged" injured party underscores that it is sufficient for a party to show that it has allegedly suffered harm in order to have sufficient interest to bring an action before a national court.

52. Secondly, the definition refers to "someone acting on behalf of one or more alleged injured parties where Union or national law provides for that possibility". This formulation allows for collective actions by a collective entity, where EU or national law provides for such possibility. An example of such a collective entity can be a consumer association. Such an association can bring an action for damages on behalf of the consumers it represents who have allegedly suffered harm caused by an infringement of competition law. The scope of this second scenario is however wider than collective actions. Reference is made to the wording "acting on behalf of *one* or *more* alleged injured parties". The inclusion of the word "one" underscores that this scenario is not limited to collective actions, but also covers the possible situation of someone acting on behalf of one alleged injured party.

53. The third scenario covers actions brought "by a natural or legal person that succeeded in the right of the alleged injured party, including the person that acquired the claim". The reference at the end of the sentence to "the person that acquired the claim" is intended to be very broad. It covers every person who acquired a claim for damages. The PDD defines a "claim for damages" as "a claim for compensation for harm caused by an infringement of competition law". There are many ways in which a person can acquire a claim under national civil law. All possible lawful manners of acquiring such a claim are covered by the third scenario. This implies that any person who acquires a claim for damages is allowed to bring an action for damages, regardless of the conditions under which he acquired such a claim, but provided that such acquisition was lawful.

Question:

54. Collective redress[32] is a mechanism that allows to group proceedings of different claimants. Collective redress encompasses both claims brought collectively or through a collective entity. Can a Member State oblige all injured parties who suffered harm caused by the same conduct to bring an action for damages through a collective entity?

Answer:

55. A Member State can foresee the possibility of collective redress. In doing so, Member States may limit the claimants who can make use of the collective redress mechanism to representative organisations.[33] For instance, Member States may limit collective redress to representative organisations acting on behalf of a specific group of allegedly injured parties, such as a consumer organisation representing a group of injured consumers.

56. However, the mechanism of collective redress contained in national law can never prevent an individual customer from exercising its individual right to bring an action for damages. Hence, a consumer cannot be obliged to bring an action for damages through a representative entity.

E. ARTICLE 2(14) PDD: CARTEL

> *"cartel" means an agreement or concerted practice between two or more competitors aimed at coordinating their competitive behaviour on the market or influencing the relevant parameters of competition through practices such as, but not limited to, the fixing or coordination of purchase or selling prices or other trading conditions, including in relation to intellectual property rights, the*

[32] On 11 June 2013 the Commission published a recommendation on collective redress setting out a series of common, non-binding principles for collective redress mechanisms in the Member States (Commission Recommendation of 11 June 2013 on common principles for injunctive and compensatory collective redress mechanisms in the Member States concerning violations of rights granted under Union Law [2013] OJ L201/60). Collective redress is defined in the Commission Recommendation as (i) a legal mechanism that ensures the possibility of claiming cessation of illegal behaviour collectively by two or more natural or legal persons or by an entity entitled to bring a representative action (injunctive collective redress); and (ii) a legal mechanism that ensures the possibility of claiming compensation collectively by two or more natural or legal persons claiming to have been harmed in a mass harm situation or by an entity entitled to bring a representative action (compensatory collective redress).

[33] For instance, in Belgium only representative organisations can act as a claimant seeking collective redress.

allocation of production or sales quotas, the sharing of markets and customers, including bid-rigging, restrictions of imports or exports or anti-competitive actions against other competitors

Question:

57. The definition of "cartel" contains a non-exhaustive list of examples. The exchange of information has not been included as an example. However, point 74 of the Horizontal Guidelines[34] states that the exchange of future prices or quantities will normally be considered and fined as cartels.[35] Does the exchange of future prices or quantities fall within the concept of cartels as defined in the PDD?

Answer:

58. The concept of a "cartel" is very familiar in EU competition law. Its definition in the PDD is (almost)[36] the same as the definition in the Leniency Notice[37] and Settlement Notice.[38] Hence, it is fair to assume that its scope throughout these three documents will be the same.

59. The notion of a "cartel" determines the scope of application of the Leniency Notice. The Leniency Notice clearly limits the possibility of submitting a leniency statement to cartel cases.[39] This is also reflected in the definitions of

---

34 Guidelines on the applicability of Article 101 of the Treaty on the Functioning of the European Union to horizontal cooperation agreements [2011] OJ C11/1.

35 Point 74 Horizontal Guidelines: "Information exchanges between competitors of individualised data regarding intended future prices or quantities should therefore be considered a restriction of competition by object. In addition, private exchanges between competitors of their individualised intentions regarding future prices or quantities would normally be considered and fined as cartels because they generally have the object of fixing prices or quantities. Information exchanges that constitute cartels not only infringe Article 101(1), but, in addition, are very unlikely to fulfil the conditions of Article 101(3)".

36 The definition of a cartel in the Leniency Notice and Settlement Notice refer to "practices such as" while the PDD refers to "practices such as, but not limited to". The added language in the PDD does not alter the meaning of the definition as both refer to a non-exhaustive list of examples.

37 Commission Notice on immunity from fines and reduction of fines in cartel cases [2006] OJ C298/17.

38 Commission Notice on the conduct of settlement procedures in view of the adoption of Decisions pursuant to Article 7 and Article 23 of Council Regulation (EC) No 1/2003 in cartel cases [2008] OJ C167/1.

39 Points 8 and 23 Leniency Notice refer to "undertakings disclosing their participation in an alleged cartel".

leniency programme[40] and leniency statement[41] in the PDD. The Settlement Notice likewise limits the possibility of settlement to cartel cases. It refers to "cooperation in (...) cartel cases"[42] and "when parties to the proceedings are prepared to acknowledge their participation in a cartel".[43] When leniency has been granted or a settlement decision has been taken by the Commission, it will be difficult for the undertakings involved to question the qualification of the conduct as a cartel in the context of the PDD.

60. An important consequence of the qualification of conduct as a cartel for the purposes of the PDD is that the presumption of harm (Article 17(2) PDD) can be relied upon by the claimants (see below, paras 240–243).

61. Currently, there is no case law at the EU level qualifying practices consisting merely in the exchange of sensitive future business information as cartels. This issue is however touched upon in the Horizontal Guidelines. The section on information exchanges in the Horizontal Guidelines deals specifically with the situation where undertakings, without entering into explicit agreements to fix prices or share markets, coordinate their market behaviour through the exchange of information. The Horizontal Guidelines do not state that the exchange of future prices or quantities qualifies as a cartel, but rather that it "would normally be considered and fined as cartels". The language in point 74 therefore does not give any definitive guidance on the legal qualification and there remains room for interpretation. It will be for the EU Courts to clarify whether or not the mere exchange of such information constitutes a cartel for the purposes of the PDD. This issue is not resolved in the PDD.[44]

---

40 Article 2(15) PDD: "'leniency programme' means a programme concerning the application of Article 101 TFEU or a corresponding provision under national law on the basis of which a participant in *a secret cartel*, independently of the other undertakings *involved in the cartel*, cooperates with an investigation of the competition authority, by voluntarily providing presentations regarding that participant's knowledge of, and role in, *the cartel* in return for which that participant receives, by decision or by a discontinuation of proceedings, immunity from, or a reduction in, fines for its *involvement in the cartel*" (emphasis added).

41 Article 2(16) PDD: "'leniency statement' means an oral or written presentation voluntarily provided by, or on behalf of, an undertaking or a natural person to a competition authority or a record thereof, describing the knowledge of that undertaking or natural person of *a cartel* and describing its role therein, which presentation was drawn up specifically for submission to the competition authority with a view to obtaining immunity or a reduction of fines under a leniency programme, not including pre-existing information" (emphasis added).

42 Point 1 Settlement Notice.

43 Point 2 Settlement Notice.

44 At national level, there has been a decision by the Spanish competition authority, Case S/0404/12 ("*AENA Commercial Services*"), which found the mere exchange of commercially sensitive information between car rental companies in several airports in Spain to constitute a violation of antitrust law. The conduct was however not qualified as a cartel.

F. ARTICLES 2(16) AND 2(19) PDD: LENIENCY STATEMENT AND IMMUNITY RECIPIENT

> *"leniency statement" means an oral or written presentation voluntarily provided by, or on behalf of, an undertaking or a natural person to a competition authority or a record thereof, describing the knowledge of that undertaking or natural person of a cartel and describing its role therein, which presentation was drawn up specifically for submission to the competition authority with a view to obtaining immunity or a reduction of fines under a leniency programme, not including pre-existing information*
>
> *"immunity recipient" means an undertaking which, or a natural person who, has been granted immunity from fines by a competition authority under a leniency programme*

Question:

62. The definitions of leniency statement and immunity recipient refer to "a natural person". At EU level, a natural person (who does not qualify as an undertaking) cannot be held liable for an infringement of competition law. Does this have any consequences at EU level for the liability of natural persons under the PDD?

Answer:

63. In several Member States, national competition law foresees the possibility of holding natural persons personally liable for an infringement of competition law. Such natural persons can, similar to undertakings, apply for leniency and receive immunity from fines. The possibility is not excluded that natural persons in such Member States may still be held liable to compensate injured parties in private damages actions. In order to ensure that natural persons, having applied for leniency or enjoying immunity, receive the same protection as undertakings under the PDD, reference is made to natural persons in the definition of the "leniency statement" and an "immunity recipient".

64. The references in these definitions are not intended to have any other consequences with regard to the liability of natural persons under the PDD.

G. ARTICLE 3 PDD: RIGHT TO FULL COMPENSATION

> *1. Member States shall ensure that any natural or legal person who has suffered harm caused by an infringement of competition law is able to claim and to obtain full compensation for that harm.*
>
> *2. Full compensation shall place a person who has suffered harm in the position in which that person would have been had the infringement of competition law not been committed. It shall therefore cover the right to compensation for actual loss and for loss of profit, plus the payment of interest.*
>
> *3. Full compensation under this Directive shall not lead to overcompensation, whether by means of punitive, multiple or other types of damages.*

Question:

65. Any person who has suffered harm caused by an infringement of competition law has a right to full compensation of the harm suffered. What damages are covered by the concept of full compensation according to Article 3 PDD?

Answer:

66. Article 3(1) PDD states that "any natural or legal person who has suffered harm caused by an infringement of competition law is able to claim and obtain full compensation for that harm". Full compensation covers the right to compensation for actual loss and for loss of profit, plus the payment of interest (Article 3(2) PDD). The three categories of compensation mentioned in the PDD are a reaffirmation of the definition of damages in the case law of the Court of Justice.[45]

67. Full compensation under EU law includes damages for *all harm* the injured party suffered as a result of the infringement, including moral damages. Member States need to lay down rules which allow the three categories of damages (actual loss, loss of profit and payment of interest) to be included in the compensation granted by the national courts.[46] The payment of interest is considered an

[45] Article 3(2) PDD relies upon the *Manfredi* case law: Joined Cases C-295/04 to C-298/04, 13 July 2006, ECLI:EU:C:2006:461, *Manfredi*, para 95: "it follows from the principle of effectiveness and the right of any individual to seek compensation for loss caused by a contract or by conduct liable to restrict or distort competition that injured persons must be able to seek compensation not only for actual loss (*damnum emergens*) but also for loss of profit (*lucrum cessans*) plus interest".

[46] Recital 12 PDD states that the three categories of damages must be included in the compensation, "irrespective of whether those categories are established separately or in combination in national law." This seems to mean that different categories of harm which are

essential part of the compensation in order to make good the fact that the damage sustained has not been compensated immediately, but only in time. As such, the passage of time between the harm and the compensation is recognised as an element of the damage in and of itself. Interest is due from the time when the harm occurred until the time when the compensation is paid (recital 6 PDD).

68. In *Kone*[47] the Court of Justice ruled in respect of compensation in case of umbrella pricing, thus clarifying the scope of the damage concept. Umbrella pricing implies that competing suppliers not participating in the cartel use the cartel as an umbrella to set prices, intentionally or unintentionally, at a higher level than they would have been able to do under competitive conditions. The effect of umbrella pricing is that also customers buying from non-participating suppliers become victims of the cartel. In *Kone,* the Court of Justice ruled that umbrella pricing is "one of the possible effects of the cartel that the members thereof cannot disregard" and affirmed that victims of umbrella pricing may obtain compensation from the members of a cartel even if they had no contractual relationship with them.[48]

Question:

69. Article 3(3) PDD states that full compensation should not lead to overcompensation. Punitive, multiple or other types of damages are prohibited by the PDD. What is exactly covered by the prohibition against overcompensation?

Answer:

70. The prohibition of overcompensation covers everything in excess of the mere compensation of harm suffered. Whether a reward falls under the concept of full compensation depends on the qualification of the damages under national law. When it is not defined as compensation for harm suffered, it is not covered and permitted by the PDD.

71. It has been argued that also restitutionary damages might lead to overcompensation.[49] Restitutionary damages or gain-based damages are a monetary remedy that is measured by reference to the profit made as a result of anti-competitive behaviour, instead of the loss suffered by an injured party. The

known in national law, such as general damages and special damages in the UK, or economic damage, personal damage and material damage in Belgian law are not relevant, as long as the injured party receives compensation for actual loss, loss of profit and payment of interest.

47 Case C-557/12, 5 June 2014, ECLI:EU:C:2014:1317, *Kone and Others*.

48 Case C-557/12, 5 June 2014, ECLI:EU:C:2014:1317, *Kone and Others*, para 34.

49 See, by analogy, *Devenish Nutrition Ltd and Others/Sanofi-Aventis SA (France) and Others* [2007] EWHC 2394 (Ch).

purpose of such damages is to deny a defendant any profit resulting from not respecting competition law, which may result in overcompensation.[50]

72. Within the EU, punitive damages are only found in the common law countries England and Wales, Ireland, Northern Ireland and the mixed system of Cyprus.[51] Restitutionary damages are only a feature in England.[52]

73. In *Cardiff Bus*[53] the UK Competition Appeal Tribunal granted exemplary damages (as punitive damages are called in the UK) to the injured party. The objective of the exemplary damages was clearly defined as being intended "to punish and deter". It can therefore be questioned whether the decision of the UK Competition Appeal Tribunal in *Cardiff Bus* would still be possible after the PDD is implemented in the UK, as such damages overcompensate the injured party.

Question:

74. National contract law often permits parties to a contract to agree upon a fixed amount that will be due in the event a party does not comply with competition law. This amount will be agreed upon in advance and stated in the contract. Does the concept of overcompensation prevent contracting parties from contractually agreeing upon such a fixed amount that the other party will have to pay in the event that party infringes competition law?

Answer:

75. Parties have the contractual freedom to agree upon a fixed amount in their contract as compensation for the damage a party will presumably suffer in the event the other party infringes competition law. Such contractual clauses are clearly permitted in the national contract laws of certain Member States.[54]

76. Whether the fixed amount that is contractually agreed upon results in overcompensation for the harm suffered depends *inter alia* on how the fixed

---

50 A. Howard, "Too little, too late? The European Commission's Legislative Proposals on Anti-Trust Damages Actions", *Journal of European Competition Law & Practice* 2013, 456–457.

51 C. Vanleenhove, "Punitive damages and European law: quo vademus?" in L. Meurkens and E. Nordin (eds.), *The Power of Punitive Damages: Is Europe Missing Out?*, Antwerp, Intersentia, 2012, 337–353.

52 UK House of Lords 27 July 2000, *Attorney General/Blake and Another* [2000] UKHL 45.

53 UK Competition Appeal Tribunal 5 July 2012, *2 Travel Group PLC (in liquidation)/Cardiff City Transport Services Limited* [2012] CAT 19.

54 Belgium: Articles 1226–1233 BW [Civil Code]; the Netherlands: Articles 6:91–6:93 BW [Civil Code]; France: Articles 1226–1233 Code Civil [Civil Code]; Germany: Articles 339–345 BGB [Civil Code].

amount is calculated. Full compensation is not a very strict concept. In most cases it is impossible to determine the exact amount of the damage suffered by the injured party. That is the reason why the PDD enables the national courts to make an estimation of the harm.[55] If the fixed amount agreed upon in the contract is based on methods of estimation that are similar to those a court would apply, the amount should not necessarily be qualified as overcompensation. However, if the fixed amount is much higher than the damages a party would receive in court proceedings, the difference risks being considered as overcompensation.

77. In summary, clauses of this nature are not by definition in conflict with the prohibition against overcompensation. It would however not be unreasonable to rely in a given case on the concept of overcompensation to argue that a fixed amount must be reduced, where such amount is clearly in excess of the full compensation that would otherwise result from court proceedings.

Question:

78. The possibility of an infringement of competition law granting benefits to the parties is not excluded. This might be the case when the infringement consists of a vertical agreement containing hardcore restrictions, which are not covered by a block exemption and cannot benefit from an individual exemption pursuant to Article 101(3) TFEU. Must the benefits received by the victim of an infringement of competition law be taken into account in the calculation of the harm caused by the injured party?

Answer:

79. The Court of Justice recognised in *Courage*[56] that "the protection of the rights guaranteed by Community law does not entail the unjust enrichment of those who enjoy them".[57] On the basis of this case law, the defendant could reasonably argue that the level of the damages claimed by an injured party for the harm suffered from an infringement of competition law should be reduced by the benefits it has received. For instance, in the case of export bans imposed by a supplier, it is not unreasonable to assume not only that the distributor suffered harm as a result of its inability to sell outside the designated areas, but also that the distributor may have gained from the fact that other distributors were

55 See Article 17(1) PDD and the Quantifying Harm Communication in para 9: "Quantification of harm in competition cases has always, by its very nature, been characterised by considerable limits to the degree of certainty and precision that can be expected. Sometimes only approximate estimates are possible".

56 Case C-453/99, 20 September 2001, ECLI:EU:C:2001:465, *Courage*, para 36.

57 Case C-453/99, 20 September 2001, ECLI:EU:C:2001:465, *Courage*, para 30.

subject to a similar restriction and have therefore not aggressively approached the territory of the claiming distributor.

H. ARTICLE 4 PDD: PRINCIPLE OF EFFECTIVENESS AND EQUIVALENCE

> *In accordance with the principle of effectiveness, Member States shall ensure that all national rules and procedures relating to the exercise of claims for damages are designed and applied in such a way that they do not render practically impossible or excessively difficult the exercise of the Union right to full compensation for harm caused by an infringement of competition law. In accordance with the principle of equivalence, national rules and procedures relating to actions for damages resulting from infringements of Article 101 or 102 TFEU shall not be less favourable to the alleged injured parties than those governing similar actions for damages resulting from infringements of national law.*

Question:

80. Reference is made in Article 4 PDD to "similar actions for damages resulting from infringements of national law". On the basis of the case law of the Court of Justice in *Manfredi,*[58] one would expect that the similarity aspect of the principle of equivalence would apply to actions for damages resulting from infringements of EU competition law and infringements of national competition law. What consequences must be attached to the fact that the PDD refers to a broader category of similar actions for damages, notably those resulting from "infringements of national law"?

Answer:

81. The last sentence of Article 4 PDD applies the general EU law principle of equivalence to private damages actions, requiring national rules and procedures not to be less favourable than those applicable to similar actions for damages resulting from infringements of national law.

---

[58] The Court ruled that "in the absence of Community rules governing the matter, it is for the domestic legal system of each Member State to designate the courts and tribunals having jurisdiction to hear actions for damages based on an infringement of the Community competition rules and to prescribe the detailed procedural rules governing those actions, provided that the provisions concerned are not less favourable than those governing *actions for damages based on an infringement of national competition rules*" (emphasis added).

82. In *Palmisani*[59] and *Courage*[60] the Court of Justice referred to the general notion of "similar domestic actions". In the PDD, the legislator clearly chose to follow this case law of the Court of Justice and therefore included "similar actions for damages resulting from infringements of national law" instead of the more limited wording contained in *Manfredi*, where the Court of Justice referred to "actions for damages resulting from infringements of national competition law".

83. It is therefore worthwhile for a private litigant to review the national procedural rules applicable to all national damages actions which can be considered similar. The reference to "similar damages actions" is open-ended and does not specify the actions that can fall under this notion. A private damages action will normally be based on the non-contractual liability of the undertaking in civil law countries and on tort law in the common law countries. It would therefore seem reasonable to consider all damages actions for non-contractual liability/tort as "similar damages actions". Hence, when more advantageous procedural rules apply to such similar national damages actions, a private litigant can rely on Article 4 PDD to claim the application of these procedural rules to its private damages action.

Question:

84. The principle of equivalence requires national rules and procedures governing private damages actions not to be less favourable than those governing similar actions for damages under national law. Does the principle of equivalence have an impact on the concepts of full compensation and overcompensation when national procedural rules applying to similar national damages actions would result in more favourable compensation levels?

Answer:

85. It could be argued that the principle of equivalence requires the level of compensation granted in private damages actions not to be lower than the level of compensation granted in similar damages actions. Hence, elements taken into account to arrive at full compensation in similar damages actions should also be included in the assessment of the full compensation awarded in private damages actions resulting from infringements of competition law.

---

59 Case C-261/95, 10 July 1997, ECLI:EU:C:1997:351, *Palmisani*, para 27.

60 Case C-453/99, 20 September 2001, ECLI:EU:C:2001:465, *Courage*, para 29.

86. However, it is unlikely that the principle of equivalence could set aside the substantive provision in the PDD such as the prohibition against overcompensation. A private litigant could therefore not rely on Article 4 PDD to obtain additional compensation on top of full compensation for the harm suffered, even if such additional compensation is available in similar damages actions under national law. Hence, penalty payments or restitutionary damages that may be available in similar damages actions, but which would overcompensate, cannot be re-introduced in a private damages action covered by the PDD via the backdoor of Article 4 PDD.

87. It appears that in practice the principle of equivalence will not really play a role in the determination of the level of the compensation. The PDD regulates this aspect strictly, which seems to leave little room for corrections (i.e. more favourable compensation falling within the notion of full compensation) based on the principle of equivalence. Its impact is more likely to be felt in the area of the relevant procedural rules that apply to actions for damages.

CHAPTER II
DISCLOSURE OF EVIDENCE

1. GENERAL CONTEXT

88. **Chapter II PDD** includes Articles 5–8 PDD and deals with different aspects of the disclosure of evidence.

89. Claimants that wish to bring an action for damages based on infringements of competition law are confronted with an information asymmetry. The evidence necessary to prove a claim for damages is often held exclusively by the opposing party or a third party[61] (recital 14 PDD). The PDD therefore creates meaningful and autonomous competence for national courts to order disclosure of evidence from parties to the proceedings and from third parties.[62]

90. The PDD seeks to impose minimum disclosure requirements (Article 5(8) PDD) which will apply in the national courts. Article 5(1) PDD provides that national courts must have the power to order the defendant or a third party to disclose relevant evidence which lies "in their control" provided that the claimant has presented a reasoned justification containing reasonably available facts and evidence sufficient to support the plausibility of its claim for damages. In order to ensure equality of arms, national courts must also be able to order the claimant or a third party to disclose relevant evidence upon request of the defendant (recital 15 PDD). This will be particularly relevant in cases where the defendant invokes a passing-on defence (Article 13 PDD).

91. National courts must be able to order disclosure of "specified items of evidence" or "relevant categories of evidence" circumscribed as precisely and as narrowly as possible on the basis of reasonably available facts set out in the

---

61 Such third parties include the competition authority that is or has been investigating the infringing behaviour that gave rise to the damages claim, E. De Smijter, "Private Enforcement" in F. Wijckmans and F. Tuytschaever (eds.), *Horizontal Agreements and Cartels in EU Competition Law*, Oxford, Oxford University Press, 2015, 359, para 8.129.

62 E. De Smijter, "Private Enforcement" in F. Wijckmans and F. Tuytschaever (eds.), *Horizontal Agreements and Cartels in EU Competition Law*, Oxford, Oxford University Press, 2015, 359, para 8.130.

reasoned justification.[63] Furthermore, disclosure of evidence under Article 5 PDD must be proportionate. Particular attention should be paid to preventing "fishing expeditions" (i.e. non-specific or overly broad searches for information unlikely to be of relevance to the parties to the proceedings) (recital 23 PDD).[64] National courts must have effective measures at their disposal to protect the disclosure of confidential information (Article 5(4) PDD). Legal privilege must also be respected (Article 5(6) PDD).

92. Where relevant evidence is not within the control of the defendant but is included in the file of a competition authority, the competition authority may be required by a national court to disclose the relevant evidence provided that it cannot reasonably be obtained from another party or from a third party (recital 29 PDD; Article 6(10) PDD).[65] When assessing the proportionality of an order to disclose information in this context, national courts must take into account the elements listed in Article 6(4) PDD (e.g. the need to safeguard the effectiveness of the public enforcement of competition law).

93. Article 6(5) PDD provides a list of categories of evidence (the so-called "grey list") national courts may order to disclose *only* after a competition authority has closed its proceedings by adopting a decision or otherwise.[66] Article 6(6) PDD provides that, for the purpose of actions for damages, national courts cannot at any time order a party or a third party to disclose leniency statements and settlement submissions.[67] Leniency statements and settlement submissions are "black-listed" categories of evidence benefiting from absolute[68] protection from

---

63 On this "threshold", see E. De Smijter, "Private Enforcement" in F. Wijckmans and F. Tuytschaever (eds.), *Horizontal Agreements and Cartels in EU Competition Law*, Oxford, Oxford University Press, 2015, 359, para 8.134.

64 E. De Smijter, "Private Enforcement" in F. Wijckmans and F. Tuytschaever (eds.), *Horizontal Agreements and Cartels in EU Competition Law*, Oxford, Oxford University Press, 2015, 359, para 8.132.

65 As Member States cannot deviate from the specifications of the PDD on the disclosure of evidence that is in the file of a competition authority, the PDD sets out a common EU framework for the access to evidence that is included in the file of the Commission or an NCA, see E. De Smijter, "Private Enforcement" in F. Wijckmans and F. Tuytschaever (eds.), *Horizontal Agreements and Cartels in EU Competition Law*, Oxford, Oxford University Press, 2015, 359, para 8.141.

66 E. De Smijter, "Private Enforcement" in F. Wijckmans and F. Tuytschaever (eds.), *Horizontal Agreements and Cartels in EU Competition Law*, Oxford, Oxford University Press, 2015, 359, paras 8.147–8.148.

67 On the definitions of "leniency statement" and "settlement submission", see *infra*.

68 The absolute protection from disclosure was a particularly controversial aspect of the PDD following the judgments of the Court of Justice in the *Pleiderer* and *Donau Chemie* cases, see E. Burrows and R. Allen, "The Likely Impact of the EU Damages Directive" in *The International Comparative Legal Guide to: Competition Litigation 2016*, 8th edition, www.iclg.co.uk/practice-areas/competition-litigation/competition-litigation-2016/1-the-likely-impact-of-the-eu-damages-directive, para 2.9. On this case law, see R. Gamble, "The European embrace of private enforcement: this time with feeling", *ECLR* 2014, 470–474.

disclosure.[69] The disclosure of evidence in the file of a competition authority that does not fall within the grey or the black list may be ordered in actions for damages at any time (Article 6(9) PDD).

94. Recital 28 PDD contains an important clarification. It states that national courts should be able, at any time, to order the disclosure of pre-existing information in the context of an action for damages. Pre-existing information is described as "evidence that exists independently of the proceedings of a competition authority".

95. In some cases, a claimant may seek disclosure of evidence from the defendant or a third party obtained via the procedure governing access to the administrative file. The PDD provides for certain limits on the use of such evidence obtained *solely* through access to the file of a competition authority (Article 7 PDD). Evidence belonging to the categories of leniency statements and settlement submissions which is obtained *solely* through such access must be deemed inadmissible in actions for damages or otherwise protected under the applicable national rules to ensure that the protection granted by Article 6(6) PDD is respected (Article 7(1) PDD). The PDD provides for a similar protection for the "grey-listed" categories of evidence until the competition authority has closed its proceedings (Article 7(2) PDD). Finally, any evidence obtained solely through access to the file of a competition authority (and which does not fall under Article 7(1) or (2) PDD) can be used in an action for damages *only* by the (natural or legal) person who obtained the evidence or the person succeeding to that person's right, including a person that acquired that person's claim (Article 7(3) PDD).

96. To prevent the destruction of relevant evidence and to ensure that court orders as to disclosure are complied with, the PDD requires that national courts are able to impose "sufficiently deterrent penalties" (recital 33 and Article 8 PDD). Such penalties should not be limited to the parties to the proceedings, but must also be available against third parties that do not comply with a disclosure order of a national court.

97. **Recitals 14–33 PDD** provide useful guidance on the provisions contained in Chapter II PDD.

---

69 E. De Smijter, "Private Enforcement" in F. Wijckmans and F. Tuytschaever (eds.), *Horizontal Agreements and Cartels in EU Competition Law*, Oxford, Oxford University Press, 2015, 359, para 8.150.

2. DISCUSSION OF RELEVANT PROVISIONS OF THE PDD

A. ARTICLE 5 PDD: DISCLOSURE OF EVIDENCE

1. Member States shall ensure that in proceedings relating to an action for damages in the Union, upon request of a claimant who has presented a reasoned justification containing reasonably available facts and evidence sufficient to support the plausibility of its claim for damages, national courts are able to order the defendant or a third party to disclose relevant evidence which lies in their control, subject to the conditions set out in this Chapter. Member States shall ensure that national courts are able, upon request of the defendant, to order the claimant or a third party to disclose relevant evidence. This paragraph is without prejudice to the rights and obligations of national courts under Regulation (EC) No 1206/2001.

2. Member States shall ensure that national courts are able to order the disclosure of specified items of evidence or relevant categories of evidence circumscribed as precisely and as narrowly as possible on the basis of reasonably available facts in the reasoned justification.

3. Member States shall ensure that national courts limit the disclosure of evidence to that which is proportionate. In determining whether any disclosure requested by a party is proportionate, national courts shall consider the legitimate interests of all parties and third parties concerned. They shall, in particular, consider:

(a) the extent to which the claim or defence is supported by available facts and evidence justifying the request to disclose evidence;

(b) the scope and cost of disclosure, especially for any third parties concerned, including preventing non-specific searches for information which is unlikely to be of relevance for the parties in the procedure;

(c) whether the evidence the disclosure of which is sought contains confidential information, especially concerning any third parties, and what arrangements are in place for protecting such confidential information.

4. Member States shall ensure that national courts have the power to order the disclosure of evidence containing confidential information where they consider it relevant to the action for damages. Member States shall ensure that, when ordering the disclosure of such information, national courts have at their disposal effective measures to protect such information.

> *5. The interest of undertakings to avoid actions for damages following an infringement of competition law shall not constitute an interest that warrants protection.*
>
> *6. Member States shall ensure that national courts give full effect to applicable legal professional privilege under Union or national law when ordering the disclosure of evidence.*
>
> *7. Member States shall ensure that those from whom disclosure is sought are provided with an opportunity to be heard before a national court orders disclosure under this Article.*
>
> *8. Without prejudice to paragraphs 4 and 7 and to Article 6, this Article shall not prevent Member States from maintaining or introducing rules which would lead to wider disclosure of evidence.*

Question:

98. Article 5(1) PDD states that Member States must ensure that national courts are able to order the defendant or "a third party" to disclose relevant evidence which lies in their control in proceedings relating to an action for damages. What is meant by the reference to "a third party"? What is meant by the reference to "relevant evidence which lies in their control"?

Answer:

99. The reference to "a third party" is very broad and covers anybody who is not a party to the damages proceedings and who may hold relevant evidence (e.g. an accountant or natural persons such as retired employees). There are some limitations that must be taken into account when ordering the disclosure of evidence by such third parties.

100. Article 5(6) PDD states that national courts must give "full effect to applicable legal professional privilege under Union *or national law* when ordering the disclosure of evidence". The addition of national law is important. Where national law provides extended protection beyond the protection available following the *Akzo* judgment,[70] such extended protection will be applicable provided that national law respects the principles of effectiveness and

[70] Case C-550/07 P, 14 September 2010, ECLI:EU:C:2010:512, *Akzo Nobel Chemicals and Akcros Chemicals/Commission.*

equivalence. A possible example is the extension of legal privilege by national law to documents prepared by in-house lawyers.[71]

101. Special care should be taken when the disclosure of confidential information is ordered (Article 5(4) PDD).

102. The PDD explicitly provides that the interest of undertakings to avoid actions for damages shall *not* constitute an interest that warrants protection (Article 5(5) PDD).

Question:

103. What is meant by the reference to "relevant evidence which lies in their control" in Article 5(1) PDD?

Answer:

104. "Lies in their control" is not defined in the PDD and will therefore be subject to what the national court finds reasonable. This "control" test exists already in a number of jurisdictions and is therefore not novel. The underlying idea is that a party to the proceedings or a third party will not have the required degree of control only if it cannot produce the evidence. This is quite a severe test as difficulties in digging up the required evidence will normally not qualify as lack of control. A refusal to produce evidence which is in the control of the party from whom it is ordered can be sanctioned (Article 8 PDD).

105. Disclosure can only be ordered where a claimant has presented a reasoned justification containing reasonably available facts and evidence sufficient to support the plausibility of its claim for damages.[72] The same test applies if the defendant formulates a request for the claimant or a third party to disclose relevant evidence.

Question:

106. What can a national court do if the third party that holds the relevant evidence is residing in a different Member State?

---

[71] Brussels Court of Appeal 5 March 2013, 2011/MR/3, *Belgacom*.

[72] R. Gamble, "The European embrace of private enforcement: this time with feeling", *ECLR* 2014, 476.

Answer:

107. Article 5(1) of the PDD specifies that it is without prejudice to the rights and obligations of national courts under Regulation 1206/2001.[73] Recital 17 PDD clarifies that the provisions of Regulation 1206/2001 apply where a court in one Member State requests a competent court in another Member State to take evidence or requests that evidence be taken directly in another Member State. Regulation 1206/2001 applies in civil and commercial matters where the court of a Member State requests the competent court of another Member State to take evidence or to take evidence directly in another Member State (Article 1 Regulation 1206/2001). Article 17 Regulation 1206/2001 sets out the rules on the direct taking of evidence.

Question:

108. Do the Member States have flexibility when transposing the rules of the disclosure of evidence into their national legislation?

Answer:

109. Article 5(8) PDD states that Member States are not prevented from maintaining or introducing rules which would lead to wider disclosure of evidence. However, such wider rules may not violate Article 5(4) (protection of confidential information), Article 5(7) (right to be heard) or Article 6 PDD (rules applicable to disclosure of evidence in the file of a competition authority). This implies, for instance, that Member States can limit in their implementing legislation the application of the proportionality standard set in Article 5(3) PDD.

B. ARTICLE 6 PDD: DISCLOSURE OF EVIDENCE INCLUDED IN THE FILE OF A COMPETITION AUTHORITY

> *1. Member States shall ensure that, for the purpose of actions for damages, where national courts order the disclosure of evidence included in the file of a competition authority, this Article applies in addition to Article 5.*
>
> *2. This Article is without prejudice to the rules and practices on public access to documents under Regulation (EC) No 1049/2001.*

73 Council Regulation (EC) No 1206/2001 of 28 May 2001 on cooperation between the courts of the Member States in the taking of evidence in civil or commercial matters [2001] OJ L174/1.

3. This Article is without prejudice to the rules and practices under Union or national law on the protection of internal documents of competition authorities and of correspondence between competition authorities.

4. When assessing, in accordance with Article 5(3), the proportionality of an order to disclose information, national courts shall, in addition, consider the following:
(a) whether the request has been formulated specifically with regard to the nature, subject matter or contents of documents submitted to a competition authority or held in the file thereof, rather than by a non-specific application concerning documents submitted to a competition authority;
(b) whether the party requesting disclosure is doing so in relation to an action for damages before a national court; and
(c) in relation to paragraphs 5 and 10, or upon request of a competition authority pursuant to paragraph 11, the need to safeguard the effectiveness of the public enforcement of competition law.

5. National courts may order the disclosure of the following categories of evidence only after a competition authority, by adopting a decision or otherwise, has closed its proceedings:
(a) information that was prepared by a natural or legal person specifically for the proceedings of a competition authority;
(b) information that the competition authority has drawn up and sent to the parties in the course of its proceedings; and
(c) settlement submissions that have been withdrawn.

6. Member States shall ensure that, for the purpose of actions for damages, national courts cannot at any time order a party or a third party to disclose any of the following categories of evidence:
(a) leniency statements; and
(b) settlement submissions.

7. A claimant may present a reasoned request that a national court access the evidence referred to in point (a) or (b) of paragraph 6 for the sole purpose of ensuring that their contents correspond to the definitions in points (16) and (18) of Article 2. In that assessment, national courts may request assistance only from the competent competition authority. The authors of the evidence in question may also have the possibility to be heard. In no case shall the national court permit other parties or third parties access to that evidence.

8. If only parts of the evidence requested are covered by paragraph 6, the remaining parts thereof shall, depending on the category under which they fall, be released in accordance with the relevant paragraphs of this Article.

9. The disclosure of evidence in the file of a competition authority that does not fall into any of the categories listed in this Article may be ordered in actions for damages at any time, without prejudice to this Article.

10. Member States shall ensure that national courts request the disclosure from a competition authority of evidence included in its file only where no party or third party is reasonably able to provide that evidence.

11. To the extent that a competition authority is willing to state its views on the proportionality of disclosure requests, it may, acting on its own initiative, submit observations to the national court before which a disclosure order is sought.

Question:

110. Article 6(6) PDD provides a high level of protection for two categories of evidence (leniency statements and settlement submissions). National courts cannot order the disclosure of such categories of evidence, not even after the proceedings have been closed.[74] Does this exceptional protection apply only to the immunity statement of the undertaking obtaining full immunity or does it apply to all leniency statements?

Answer:

111. The protection of Article 6(6) PDD applies to all leniency statements, whether this relates to an application for immunity from fines or a reduction of fines.

112. Article 2(16) PDD defines a "leniency statement" as a presentation of the "knowledge" of an undertaking or natural person of a cartel and describing its role therein.[75] Hence, a leniency statement covers the presentation, in a voluntary way, of an undertaking's or a natural person's knowledge of a cartel

[74] E. De Smijter, "Private Enforcement" in F. Wijckmans and F. Tuytschaever (eds.), *Horizontal Agreements and Cartels in EU Competition Law*, Oxford, Oxford University Press, 2015, 359, para 8.150.

[75] Article 2(16) PDD: "'leniency statement' means an oral or written presentation voluntarily provided by, or on behalf of, an undertaking or a natural person to a competition authority or a record thereof, describing the knowledge of that undertaking or natural person of a cartel and describing its role therein, which presentation was drawn up specifically for submission to the competition authority with a view to obtaining immunity or a reduction of fines under a leniency programme, not including pre-existing information".

to the competition authority. This definition is not limited to an application for immunity.

113. A "cartel" is defined in Article 2(14) PDD as an agreement or concerted practice between two or more competitors aimed at coordinating their competitive behaviour on the market or influencing the relevant parameters of competition.[76] Article 2(14) PDD contains a non-exhaustive list of relevant practices that are covered by the definition of a "cartel".

114. The definition of a "leniency statement" in Article 2(16) PDD explicitly refers to an oral or written presentation "drawn up specifically for submission to the competition authority with a view to obtaining immunity or a reduction of fines under a leniency programme". It therefore makes a clear link with a leniency programme. The term "leniency programme" is defined in Article 2(15) PDD.[77]

115. In order to appreciate the scope of the exception made for leniency statements in Article 6(6) PDD, it is important to make a combined reading of the definitions of leniency statement, cartels and leniency programme. For the purposes of Article 6(6) PDD, a leniency statement made in connection with a leniency programme will *only* be covered by the prohibition on disclosure *if* the leniency statement relates to a *secret* cartel. The secrecy requirement is not included in the definitions of a "cartel" or a "leniency statement", but is included in the definition of a "leniency programme". Through the reference to a "leniency programme" in the definition of a "leniency statement", it is however clear that leniency statements will only benefit from the protection offered by Article 6(6) PDD if they relate to secret cartels and not just cartels.

116. Leniency programmes in some Member States provide for leniency for horizontal practices that do not necessarily qualify as secret cartels or even for other types of infringements (e.g. restrictive vertical practices). The reference

[76] Article 2(14) PDD: "'cartel' means an agreement or concerted practice between two or more competitors aimed at coordinating their competitive behaviour on the market or influencing the relevant parameters of competition through practices such as, but not limited to, the fixing or coordination of purchase or selling prices or other trading conditions, including in relation to intellectual property rights, the allocation of production or sales quotas, the sharing of markets and customers, including bid-rigging, restrictions of imports or exports or anti-competitive actions against other competitors".

[77] Article 2(15) PDD: "'leniency programme' means a programme concerning the application of Article 101 TFEU or a corresponding provision under national law on the basis of which a participant in a secret cartel, independently of the other undertakings involved in the cartel, cooperates with an investigation of the competition authority, by voluntarily providing presentations regarding that participant's knowledge of, and role in, the cartel in return for which that participant receives, by decision or by a discontinuation of proceedings, immunity from, or a reduction in, fines for its involvement in the cartel".

to secret cartels in the PDD is not intended to harmonise leniency programmes across the Member States. Member States can continue to apply their own definitions of the terms "cartel", "leniency programme" and "leniency statement" to competition law cases that are purely internal and have no link to EU competition law. For the purposes of the PDD, however, the combined reading of the definitions limits the prohibition of disclosure to leniency statements made in relation to secret cartels. Statements made in relation to leniency programmes for other kinds of infringements are not on the black list of Article 6(6) PDD, meaning that their disclosure can at best be delayed pursuant to Article 6(5) PDD until the closure of the administrative proceedings.

117. Recital 26 PDD specifies that the exemption from disclosure should apply also to *verbatim* quotations from leniency statements or settlement submissions included in other documents.

Question:

118. Does the exclusion of leniency statements in Article 6(6) PDD cover all of the documents accompanying such statements?

Answer:

119. The definition of a "leniency statement" excludes pre-existing information. Pre-existing information is defined as "evidence that exists irrespective of the proceedings of a competition authority, whether or not such information is in the file of a competition authority" (Article 2(17) PDD). The exclusion of pre-existing information implies that the protection offered by Article 6(6) PDD only relates to the presentation in the context of a leniency programme describing the knowledge and role of an undertaking or a natural person who participated in a secret cartel. All other documents (including the exhibits with contemporaneous evidence) can therefore be disclosed.

Question:

120. Article 6(5)(c) PDD contains a list of "grey" categories of evidence, i.e. categories of evidence that can only be ordered to be disclosed after the competition authority has closed its proceedings. The grey list includes "settlement submissions that have been withdrawn". What is meant by this reference?

Answer:

121. A "settlement submission" is defined in Article 2(18) PDD.[78] Within the context of the Settlement Notice a settlement submission cannot be withdrawn by the parties. The Settlement Notice contained the term "withdrawn" in relation to the end of the settlement procedure when the Commission considers that the settlement submission does not correspond to what had been agreed under the settlement procedure (points 27 and 29 of the Settlement Notice). The Settlement Notice has recently been reviewed to align it with the PDD. The wording "withdrawn" has been changed to "disregarded" in order to avoid any confusion.[79] If, under the Settlement Notice, the Commission decides to end the settlement procedure, the settlement submission will *not* qualify as a withdrawal under Article 6(5)(c) PDD.

122. However, the withdrawal of a settlement submission is provided for in the settlement programmes of some of the Member States. Article 6(5)(c) PDD is relevant for withdrawals under such national settlement programmes. As stated above, it will have no significance when it comes to settlement submissions made in the context of Commission proceedings.

Question:

123. What is the status of documents that are submitted in order to negotiate a settlement but that technically do not amount to settlement submissions, such as non-papers? Do these types of documents fall under Article 6(5) PDD (grey list) or Article 6(6) PDD (black list)?

Answer:

124. A settlement submission describes the undertaking's acknowledgement of, or its renunciation to dispute, its participation in an infringement of competition law and its responsibility for that infringement of competition law (Article 2(18) PDD). A so-called non-paper would not fall under this definition as it would typically not include an acknowledgment of participation, but would rather address specific issues such as the value of sales or comments on the case overview provided by the Commission. Therefore, a non-paper would fall under

---

78 Article 2(18) PDD: "'settlement submission' means a voluntary presentation by, or on behalf of, an undertaking to a competition authority describing the undertaking's acknowledgement of, or its renunciation to dispute, its participation in an infringement of competition law and its responsibility for that infringement of competition law, which was drawn up specifically to enable the competition authority to apply a simplified or expedited procedure".

79 Amendments to the Commission Notice on the conduct of settlement procedures in view of the adoption of Decisions pursuant to Article 7 and Article 23 of Council Regulation (EC) No 1/2003 in cartel cases [2015] OJ C256/2.

Article 6(5)(a) PDD rather than under Article 6(6)(b) PDD. Hence, a non-paper is not protected from disclosure if the non-paper does not meet the definition of a settlement submission.

Question:

125. Does the protection offered by Article 6(6) PDD extend to subsequent documents that refer to earlier settlement submissions or leniency statements?

Answer:

126. Recital 26 PDD provides that the "exemption [of disclosure] should also apply to *verbatim* quotations from leniency statements or settlement submissions included in other documents". The exemption however only applies to the *verbatim* statements, so not to the entire document containing a *verbatim* statement, or to excerpts of documents paraphrasing the content of settlement submissions or leniency statements.

Question:

127. Article 6(5) PDD provides that the evidence listed in that paragraph can only be disclosed "after a competition authority, by adopting a decision or otherwise, has closed its proceedings". Does the adoption of a "decision" include the decision to accept commitments?

Answer:

128. A logical reading of Article 6(5) PDD implies that anything that legally closes the proceedings triggers the end of the protection from disclosure under Article 6(5) PDD. This includes a decision to accept commitments.

C. ARTICLE 7 PDD: LIMITS ON THE USE OF EVIDENCE OBTAINED SOLELY THROUGH ACCESS TO THE FILE OF A COMPETITION AUTHORITY

> *1. Member States shall ensure that evidence in the categories listed in Article 6(6) which is obtained by a natural or legal person solely through access to the file of a competition authority is either deemed to be inadmissible in actions for damages or is otherwise protected under the applicable national rules to ensure the full effect of the limits on the disclosure of evidence set out in Article 6.*

2. Member States shall ensure that, until a competition authority has closed its proceedings by adopting a decision or otherwise, evidence in the categories listed in Article 6(5) which is obtained by a natural or legal person solely through access to the file of that competition authority is either deemed to be inadmissible in actions for damages or is otherwise protected under the applicable national rules to ensure the full effect of the limits on the disclosure of evidence set out in Article 6.

3. Member States shall ensure that evidence which is obtained by a natural or legal person solely through access to the file of a competition authority and which does not fall under paragraph 1 or 2, can be used in an action for damages only by that person or by a natural or legal person that succeeded to that person's rights, including a person that acquired that person's claim.

Question:

129. Do the principles contained in Article 7 PDD also apply to evidence obtained through access to the file in the context of the administrative proceedings before the competition authority?

Answer:

130. Article 7 PDD imposes limits on the use of evidence obtained *solely* through access to the file of a competition authority. This includes information obtained from the file of a competition authority, including access as a party to the public enforcement proceedings (e.g. the addressee of a statement of objections has a right to access the file).[80] The information obtained through such access (e.g. to enable a party to exercise its right of defence) can be used for the purposes of judicial proceedings involving the application of Articles 101 and 102 TFEU. This includes using such documents in the context of an antitrust damages action.[81] Recital 31 PDD underscores that any natural or legal person that obtains evidence through access to the file of a competition authority should be able to use that evidence for the purposes of an action for damages to which it is a party.

131. During access to the file in a public enforcement proceeding, access may be granted to information that is not or not yet disclosable by a national court

[80] E. De Smijter, "Private Enforcement" in F. Wijckmans and F. Tuytschaever (eds.), *Horizontal Agreements and Cartels in EU Competition Law*, Oxford, Oxford University Press, 2015, 359, para 8.156.

[81] E. De Smijter, "Private Enforcement" in F. Wijckmans and F. Tuytschaever (eds.), *Horizontal Agreements and Cartels in EU Competition Law*, Oxford, Oxford University Press, 2015, 359, para 8.156.

under the PDD. To avoid the circumvention of the protection from disclosure in an action for damages by the use of information that was legally obtained in the course of public enforcement proceedings, the PDD "mirrors" the protection against disclosure in Article 6 PDD by limiting the use of that information (Articles 7(1) and (2) PDD). The limitation is formulated as the "inadmissibility" of such information as evidence in an action for damages: the use of black-listed information (Article 6(6) PDD) is always inadmissible, whereas the use of grey-listed information (Article 6(5) PDD) is inadmissible until the competition authority has closed its proceedings.[82]

Question:

132. Who can make use of the information obtained through access to the file?

Answer:

133. Article 7(3) PDD limits the use of information obtained through access to the file to the person who obtained this information or the person who succeeded in its rights, including the person who acquired its claim. This provision prevents the mere commercialisation of the information[83] that was obtained through access to the file.[84]

D. ARTICLE 8 PDD: PENALTIES

> *1. Member States shall ensure that national courts are able effectively to impose penalties on parties, third parties and their legal representatives in the event of any of the following:*
> *(a) their failure or refusal to comply with the disclosure order of any national court;*
> *(b) their destruction of relevant evidence;*
> *(c) their failure or refusal to comply with the obligations imposed by a national court order protecting confidential information;*
> *(d) their breach of the limits on the use of evidence provided for in this Chapter.*

82 E. De Smijter, "Private Enforcement" in F. Wijckmans and F. Tuytschaever (eds.), *Horizontal Agreements and Cartels in EU Competition Law*, Oxford, Oxford University Press, 2015, 359, para 8.157.

83 See also recital 32 PDD which states that evidence obtained from a competition authority should not become an object of trade.

84 E. De Smijter, "Private Enforcement" in F. Wijckmans and F. Tuytschaever (eds.), *Horizontal Agreements and Cartels in EU Competition Law*, Oxford, Oxford University Press, 2015, 359, para 8.158.

> *2. Member States shall ensure that the penalties that can be imposed by national courts are effective, proportionate and dissuasive. The penalties available to national courts shall include, with regard to the behaviour of a party to proceedings for an action for damages, the possibility to draw adverse inferences, such as presuming the relevant issue to be proven or dismissing claims and defences in whole or in part, and the possibility to order the payment of costs.*

Question:

134. Article 8(1) PDD refers to penalties imposed on "parties, third parties and their legal representatives". How must "legal representatives" be understood? Can a managing director or an executive board member be held liable if employees commit offences listed in Article 8(1)(a)–(d) PDD?

Answer:

135. Employees cannot violate EU competition law since they are not "undertakings" for the purposes of Articles 101 and 102 TFEU. If an employee commits one of the offences listed in Article 8(1)(a)–(d) PDD, the company will be the "party" to which Article 8(1) PDD refers.

136. Legal representatives refer to physical persons who can legally represent a legal entity. Managers or executive board members may therefore qualify as legal representatives of the company. If such legal representatives commit offences listed in Article 8(1)(a)–(d) PDD, the law of the Member States must provide for the possibility of sanctions. However, it remains a faculty for the national courts ("are able") and the PDD does not prescribe that such sanctions must be imposed by national courts. If it is established that a party, a third party or a legal representative has committed one of the offences, the court is not obliged, but has the option, to impose a sanction. The national law of the Member States can also provide for conditions which have to be fulfilled in order to hold legal representatives responsible.

Question:

137. Do "legal representative" and/or "third party" in Article 8(1) PDD cover law firms or lawyers representing undertakings which are involved in a private damages claim? Can a lawyer be sanctioned for the refusal, based on legal professional privilege, to comply with a disclosure order as envisaged by Article 8(1)(a) PDD?

Answer:

138. The notion of "third party" must be given the widest possible interpretation and, as such, also encompasses law firms that are in any way connected to the undertaking. The PDD therefore does not exclude that law firms can be held liable for the offences listed in Article 8(1) PDD.

139. As to the refusal to comply with a disclosure order of a national court, Article 5(6) PDD provides for an exception for legal professional privilege. Due to Article 5(6) PDD, a court cannot order a lawyer representing an undertaking to disclose information covered by legal professional privilege. Hence, the refusal by a lawyer to disclose information which is covered by legal professional privilege will not constitute an offence for the purposes of Article 8(1)(a) PDD. Such privilege will not extend to the destruction of evidence, which may amount to misconduct on the part of the lawyer.

Question:

140. Does a Member State sufficiently implement the PDD if it copies the examples of penalties listed in the last sentence of Article 8(2) PDD?

Answer:

141. The examples of penalties in Article 8(2) PDD are mainly penalties which target the parties ("with regard to the behaviour of a party to proceedings for an action for damages") and not so much third parties or legal representatives. It could be argued that implementation would be sufficient if only these examples of penalties were used, as long as they are used in an effective, proportionate and dissuasive way.

Question:

142. Can a European manager be held liable when all the relevant information and documents have been transferred to another branch of the company outside the EU (e.g. the US or China) and that branch refuses to disclose the information and documents?

Answer:

143. If the decision to transfer the documents *follows* the opening of an EU investigation, the transfer has made the evidence no longer available to a court. Depending on the circumstances, the European manager risks being found to have made the documents unavailable under Article 8(1) PDD. If the decision to transfer documents was taken *prior* to the opening of an investigation, it is up to

the national court to decide whether the transfer genuinely occurred in *tempore non suspecto* and to assess the legality of such transfer under the applicable national rules.

144. The first draft proposal of the PDD provided, among other things, clear time limits until which evidence had to be kept. Such time limits have been taken out by the legislator in the final PDD as the imposition of time limits was considered to be over-regulating.

Question:

145. Is the sanction of drawing "adverse inferences" mandatory or compulsory?

Answer:

146. Article 8(2) PDD states that the penalties "shall include" the possibility of drawing adverse inferences. Hence, this sanction is mandatory and constitutes a minimum that needs to be provided in national law. It is up to national law to provide for the conditions which have to be met in order to draw adverse inferences and to specify what adverse inferences can be drawn. It is also up to the national court to assess the gravity of the facts at hand. The aim of Article 8(2) PDD was to avoid a situation where one could commit the offences listed in Article 8(1) PDD and only pay a fine.

CHAPTER III

EFFECT OF NATIONAL DECISIONS, LIMITATION PERIODS, JOINT AND SEVERAL LIABILITY

1. GENERAL CONTEXT

147. **Chapter III PDD** introduces measures aimed at assisting injured parties to claim and obtain full compensation for the harm suffered due to a competition law infringement. The relevant provisions are Articles 9–11 PDD.

148. Article 9 PDD establishes the effect of final infringement decisions adopted by NCAs or national review courts in the framework of subsequent actions for damages before national courts. The following definitions in Article 2 PDD are relevant for the purposes of this provision:

- An "infringement decision" means "a decision of a competition authority or review court that finds an infringement of competition law" (Article 2(11) PDD).

- A "final infringement decision" means "an infringement decision that cannot be, or that can no longer be, appealed by ordinary means" (Article 2(12) PDD).

- An "NCA" is defined as "an authority designated by a Member State pursuant to Article 35 of Regulation (EC) No 1/2003, as being responsible for the application of Articles 101 and 102 TFEU" (Article 2(7) PDD).

- A "review court" is defined as "a national court that is empowered by ordinary means of appeal to review decisions of a national competition authority or to review judgments pronouncing on those decisions, irrespective of whether that court itself has the power to find an infringement of competition law" (Article 2(10) PDD).

- A "national court" means "a court or tribunal of a Member State within the meaning of Article 267 TFEU" (Article 2(9) PDD).

149. Article 10 PDD sets minimum requirements for Member States with regard to limitation periods for bringing actions for damages.

150. Article 11 PDD establishes the principle of joint and several liability, allowing an injured party to require compensation from any of the infringing undertakings until it has received full compensation. The principle of joint and several liability may cause an infringing undertaking to contribute more than its share in the harm. Article 11 PDD therefore also addresses the right to obtain contribution from co-infringing undertakings.

151. **Recitals 34–38 PDD** provide more context on the rules introduced in Chapter III PDD.

2. DISCUSSION OF RELEVANT PROVISIONS OF THE PDD

A. ARTICLE 9 PDD: EFFECT OF NATIONAL DECISIONS

> *1. Member States shall ensure that an infringement of competition law found by a final decision of a national competition authority or by a review court is deemed to be irrefutably established for the purposes of an action for damages brought before their national courts under Article 101 or 102 TFEU or under national competition law.*
>
> *2. Member States shall ensure that where a final decision referred to in paragraph 1 is taken in another Member State that final decision may, in accordance with national law, be presented before their national courts as at least prima facie evidence that an infringement of competition law has occurred and, as appropriate, may be assessed along with any other evidence adduced by the parties.*
>
> *3. This Article is without prejudice to the rights and obligations of national courts under Article 267 TFEU.*

Question:

152. Article 9(1) PDD establishes the principle that a final decision of an NCA or a review court finding a competition law infringement is deemed to be irrefutably established for the purposes of an action for damages brought before their national courts under EU or national competition law. How far does this principle extend? To what extent does a final decision have a binding impact?

Answer:

153. By stating that a competition law infringement established by a final decision of an NCA or a review court is deemed irrefutably established, Article 9(1) PDD aims to prevent a situation where the finding of an infringement would be re-litigated in subsequent actions for damages. As a result, claimants do not have to prove the scope of the infringement again and can therefore concentrate on proving causation and the quantum of the damages. This provision was created to enhance legal certainty, to avoid inconsistency in the application of Articles 101 and 102 TFEU, to increase the effectiveness and procedural efficiency of actions for damages and to foster the functioning of the internal market for undertakings and consumers (recital 34 PDD).

154. According to recital 34 PDD, the binding effect of the decision finding an infringement covers only "the nature of the infringement and its material, personal, temporal and territorial scope as determined by the competition authority or review court in the exercise of its jurisdiction". The binding effect thus covers all aspects of the infringement. However, it is unclear to what extent this also covers the underlying evidence that is contained in the decision and which supports or is constitutive to the finding of the infringement. This means that national judges are not bound by other findings of fact contained in the decision. Where the nature and the scope of the infringement cannot be challenged before the civil judge, some findings of fact can be subject to further discussion. Infringers can, for example, point to the existence of evidence that, considered together with evidence contained in the file, proves that no harm was effectively caused to a claimant. It should however be emphasised that this argumentation can only be used as far as the issues of causation or harm are concerned. Infringers cannot, as far as the illegality of the conduct is concerned, re-open the debate.

Question:

155. Article 9(2) PDD deals with the situation in which a final infringement decision is taken in a different Member State than the Member State where the action for damages is brought. In this case, Article 9(2) PDD ensures that the final decision given in another Member State may be presented before national courts at least as *prima facie* evidence that a breach of competition law has occurred and may be assessed along with any other evidence adduced by the parties. What does this provision involve in practice?

Answer:

156. As set out in the response to the previous question, a final infringement decision of an NCA (or national review court) constitutes full proof of that

infringement before the courts of the same Member State (Article 9(1) PDD). The draft PDD originally assigned the same binding effect also to decisions adopted by NCAs of other Member States. This proved to be a controversial issue during the debates on the proposed PDD and a compromise had to be found. Article 9(2) PDD therefore now provides that infringement findings adopted by an NCA in one Member State will only constitute "at least *prima facie* evidence" that an infringement has occurred, rather than legally binding proof of the infringement. The infringement decision will then have to be assessed "along with any other evidence adduced by the parties".

157. The fact that Article 9(2) PDD provides that an infringement decision of an NCA should *at least* be seen as *prima facie* evidence appears to imply that national courts are allowed to attach more value to it and are in any event not allowed to ignore the decision. It remains to be seen how much weight will be given in practice by national courts to decisions by NCAs of other Member States. The compromise position reached in Article 9(2) PDD leaves national courts with a considerable degree of discretion and, given the wording of Article 9(2) PDD, it seems unlikely that a national court will accept an infringement decision of an NCA of another Member State as binding proof of liability without looking in detail at the facts and reaching its own conclusions on the issue of whether there has been an infringement.[85] That being said, Member States are of course free to also give binding effect to decisions by NCAs of other Member States.

B. ARTICLE 10 PDD: LIMITATION PERIODS

1. Member States shall, in accordance with this Article, lay down rules applicable to limitation periods for bringing actions for damages. Those rules shall determine when the limitation period begins to run, the duration thereof and the circumstances under which it is interrupted or suspended.

2. Limitation periods shall not begin to run before the infringement of competition law has ceased and the claimant knows, or can reasonably be expected to know:
(a) of the behaviour and the fact that it constitutes an infringement of competition law;
(b) of the fact that the infringement of competition law caused harm to it; and
(c) the identity of the infringer.

[85] E. Burrows and R. Allen, "The Likely Impact of the EU Damages Directive" in *The International Comparative Legal Guide to: Competition Litigation 2016*, 8th edition, www.iclg.co.uk/practice-areas/competition-litigation/competition-litigation-2016/1-the-likely-impact-of-the-eu-damages-directive, para 3.4.

> *3. Member States shall ensure that the limitation periods for bringing actions for damages are at least five years.*
>
> *4. Member States shall ensure that a limitation period is suspended or, depending on national law, interrupted, if a competition authority takes action for the purpose of the investigation or its proceedings in respect of an infringement of competition law to which the action for damages relates. The suspension shall end at the earliest one year after the infringement decision has become final or after the proceedings are otherwise terminated.*

Question:

158. Article 10(2)(a) PDD states that limitation periods shall not begin to run before the infringement has ceased and the claimant knows, or can reasonably be expected to know, "of the behaviour and the fact that it constitutes an infringement of competition law". Does this refer to the legal qualification of the conduct? In the case of a cartel, how much more of a burden does this amount to?

Answer:

159. Article 10(2)(a) PDD imposes a double condition. First, the claimant must be aware of the behaviour. This relates to the factual aspects of the conduct of the infringer. Second, the claimant must be aware of the fact that such behaviour amounts to an infringement of Article 101 or 102 TFEU. This relates to the legal qualification of the conduct. The reference to "an infringement of competition law" implies that it suffices that the claimant is aware or can reasonably be expected to know that an infringement of Article 101 or 102 TFEU is involved. Whether the infringement qualifies furthermore as a cartel or any other more specific type of infringement is not required.

Question:

160. Article 10(4) PDD foresees the suspension or, depending on national law, interruption of the limitation period if a competition authority takes action for the purposes of the investigation or its proceedings in respect of an infringement of competition law to which the action for damages relates. Such suspension (or interruption) shall, according to Article 10(4) PDD, "end at the earliest one year after the infringement decision has become final or after the proceedings are otherwise terminated". Should "has become final" be understood as a "final infringement decision" in the sense of Article 2(12) PDD?

Answer:

161. Article 10(4) PDD does not specify what is meant by an infringement decision becoming "final". A fair reading of this provision implies however that this language must be interpreted as referring to a final infringement decision (as defined in Article 2(12) PDD).[86]

C. ARTICLE 11 PDD: JOINT AND SEVERAL LIABILITY

1. Member States shall ensure that undertakings which have infringed competition law through joint behaviour are jointly and severally liable for the harm caused by the infringement of competition law; with the effect that each of those undertakings is bound to compensate for the harm in full, and the injured party has the right to require full compensation from any of them until he has been fully compensated.

2. By way of derogation from paragraph 1, Member States shall ensure that, without prejudice to the right of full compensation as laid down in Article 3, where the infringer is a small or medium-sized enterprise (SME) as defined in Commission Recommendation 2003/361/EC, the infringer is liable only to its own direct and indirect purchasers where:
(a) its market share in the relevant market was below 5% at any time during the infringement of competition law; and
(b) the application of the normal rules of joint and several liability would irretrievably jeopardize its economic viability and cause its assets to lose all their value.

3. The derogation laid down in paragraph 2 shall not apply where:
(a) the SME has led the infringement of competition law or has coerced other undertakings to participate therein; or
(b) the SME has previously been found to have infringed competition law.

4. By way of derogation from paragraph 1, Member States shall ensure that an immunity recipient is jointly and severally liable as follows:
(a) to its direct or indirect purchasers or providers; and
(b) to other injured parties only where full compensation cannot be obtained from the other undertakings that were involved in the same infringement of competition law.

[86] T. De Meese, "Private Enforcement" in F. Wijckmans and F. Tuytschaever (eds.), *Horizontal Agreements and Cartels in EU Competition Law*, Oxford, Oxford University Press, 2015, 341, para 8.43.

Member States shall ensure that any limitation period applicable to cases under this paragraph is reasonable and sufficient to allow injured parties to bring such actions.

5. Member States shall ensure that an infringer may recover a contribution from any other infringer, the amount of which shall be determined in the light of their relative responsibility for the harm caused by the infringement of competition law. The amount of contribution of an infringer which has been granted immunity from fines under a leniency programme shall not exceed the amount of the harm it caused to its own direct or indirect purchasers or providers.

6. Member States shall ensure that, to the extent the infringement of competition law caused harm to injured parties other than the direct or indirect purchasers or providers of the infringers, the amount of any contribution from an immunity recipient to other infringers shall be determined in the light of its relative responsibility for that harm.

Question:

162. Article 11(1) PDD states that undertakings which have infringed competition law through joint behaviour are jointly and severally liable for the harm caused by the infringement of competition law. Reference is made to the concept of "through joint behaviour". What conduct is covered by this concept? Can vertical agreements also be covered by this concept?

Answer:

163. The fact that an undertaking is held jointly and severally liable has important consequences for the undertakings involved. It means that all injured parties who suffered harm caused by an infringement of competition law can ask for full compensation from any undertaking involved in the infringement. This is the case irrespective of whether the party against whom the damages claim is addressed did itself cause any harm to the injured party (e.g. because there was no supply relationship between such infringer and the injured party claiming compensation).

164. This means in practice that injured parties can address their claim to the most solvent undertaking involved in the infringement. That undertaking risks facing claims in all 28 Member States and even in Member States where it has not carried out any business activities.

165. It is therefore important to understand when undertakings can be held jointly and severally liable. The principle only applies to undertakings that have infringed competition law "through joint behaviour". There will be joint behaviour only when the infringement was committed by *more than one* undertaking.

166. Cartels and other agreements or concerted practices by undertakings falling under Article 101 TFEU necessarily involve more than one undertaking and, as such, fall within the concept of "through joint behaviour". This concept therefore covers horizontal as well as vertical agreements. As a consequence, a distributor which surrenders to commercial pressure from its supplier by adhering to the prices imposed on it and which is found to have infringed Article 101 TFEU can also be held jointly and severally liable to all injured parties who suffered harm caused by such infringement.[87]

Question:

167. The rules of jurisdiction within the EU determine the relevant forum in which a private damages action should be brought. Infringements of competition law often cause harm to many consumers. As such, multiple private damages actions could be brought. Is there any form of coordination between the different damages cases brought throughout the EU?

Answer:

168. The Brussels I bis Regulation[88] contains rules governing jurisdictional issues within the EU. On the basis of Article 7(2) Brussels I bis Regulation[89] an undertaking can "in matters relating to tort, delict or quasi-delict, [be sued] in the courts for the place where the harmful event occurred or may occur".

169. The Court of Justice recently confirmed in *CDC Hydrogen Peroxide*[90] that, with regard to private damages actions resulting from competition law, the reference to "the place where the harmful event occurred or may occur" in Article 7(2) Brussels I bis Regulation means that an action can be brought "before the courts of the place in which the cartel was definitively concluded or, as the case may be, the place in which one agreement in particular was concluded which is identifiable as the sole causal event giving rise to the loss

---

87 When the distributor falls under the definition of an SME, he might be exempted from this general principle (see below, paras 171–173).

88 Regulation (EU) No 1215/2012 of 12 December 2012 of the European Parliament and of the Council on jurisdiction and the recognition and enforcement of judgments in civil and commercial matters [2012] OJ L351/1.

89 Former Article 5(3) Brussels I Regulation.

90 Case C-352/13, 21 May 2015, ECLI:EU:C:2015:335, *CDC Hydrogen Peroxide.*

allegedly suffered, or before the courts of the place where its own registered office is located".[91]

170. The Brussels I bis Regulation leaves the claimant with a choice as to where to bring its action irrespective of where other damages actions are brought. The Brussels I bis Regulation does not contain any provision that requires the concentration of damages actions throughout the EU. When several claimants bring damages actions, several parallel cases may be pending. This obviously entails a risk of conflicting outcomes. This risk is however not unique to damages actions relating to infringements of competition law, but arises in all tort cases where multiple infringers and multiple injured parties are involved.

Question:

171. Article 11(2)–(3) PDD exempts an SME from being jointly and severally liable for harm caused by an infringement of competition law. This derogation does not apply when the SME led the infringement or when the SME has previously been found to have infringed competition law. Which infringements of competition law will be taken into account for determining that the SME qualifies as a repeat offender in the sense of Article 11(3)(b) PDD?

Answer:

172. The general principle included in the PDD is joint and several liability for undertakings which have infringed competition law through joint behaviour. An exception to this general principle is foreseen for SMEs. The rationale for this exception is to avoid SMEs having to compensate all the harm that was caused by the infringement of competition law (including harm caused by other infringers). Such an obligation can have very serious financial consequences for SMEs.

173. The exception contained in Article 11(2) PDD does not apply if (i) the SME was the leader/coercer of the infringement or (ii) the SME has previously been found to have infringed competition law (Article 11(3) PDD). This second point is formulated in broad terms. Hence, every infringement – even the least serious – of competition law previously committed by an SME prevents the SME from enjoying the derogation contained in Article 11(2) PDD. No limitation period has been included. As such, minor infringements committed even 20 or 30 years ago could still have an impact on an SME's financial liability towards the injured parties. The wide interpretation of the notion "infringement of competition law" and the fact that no limitation period is included therefore seriously limits the protection foreseen for SMEs.

---

91 Case C-352/13, 21 May 2015, ECLI:EU:C:2015:335, *CDC Hydrogen Peroxide*, para 56.

Question:

174. Article 11(4) PDD contains an exception to the general principle of joint and several liability for immunity recipients. Injured parties other than the direct or indirect purchasers or providers of the immunity recipient will only be able to obtain full compensation from the immunity recipient, where such compensation cannot be obtained from the other undertakings involved in the same infringement of competition law. What is the exact meaning of the wording "cannot be obtained"?

Answer:

175. Immunity recipients who are being sued by direct or indirect purchasers or providers of other infringing undertakings will not have to grant compensation as long as such claimants can still obtain compensation from the other undertakings involved. An immunity recipient could therefore invoke Article 11(4) PDD as a defence argument in private litigation.

176. The reasoning underlying this exception for immunity recipients is twofold: (i) immunity recipients play a key role in exposing secret cartels, thereby often mitigating the harm which could have been caused had the infringement continued, and (ii) the decision of competition authorities is likely to become final for the immunity recipient at an earlier stage than for some of the other infringing undertakings (which are more likely to contest the decision). The immunity recipient is therefore exposed to earlier (follow-on) damages actions and risks having to compensate the injured parties in full while other infringers are still involved in possible appeal proceedings against the decision of the Commission or the NCA (recital 38 PDD).

177. The immunity recipient is however not entirely protected from claims by other injured parties. The protection of immunity recipients should not interfere with the duly established right in EU law of an injured party to be awarded full compensation. The proposed limitation on the immunity recipient's liability is therefore not absolute. The immunity recipient remains fully liable as a last-resort debtor if the injured parties are unable to obtain full compensation from the other infringers.[92]

178. Article 11(4)(b) PDD refers to the situation where full compensation "cannot be obtained" from the other undertakings involved. Member States

92 Explanatory memorandum in the Proposal for a Directive of the European Parliament and of the Council on certain rules governing actions for damages under national law for infringements of the competition law provisions of the Member States and of the European Union, COM(2013) 404, 11.06.2013, 16–17.

have to make sure that injured parties can still claim compensation from the immunity recipient as soon as they are aware that they cannot secure full compensation from the co-cartelists.[93] The PDD does not contain any guidance on when it becomes impossible for a claimant to obtain compensation from the other infringers.

179. It remains uncertain whether the impossibility for claimants must be seen as a legal bar or a practical impediment to obtaining compensation.[94] On the basis of the wording "cannot be obtained" and "at the time they have become aware that they cannot obtain full compensation from the co-cartelists"[95] in Article 11(4) PDD, obtaining a judgment first as proof that no full compensation can be obtained does not seem to be required. The language in Article 11(4) PDD is broadly phrased and clearly leaves room for interpretation. It will therefore be for the national judge to decide at what point it is reasonable to accept that no other undertaking will compensate the injured party.

Question:

180. Article 11(5) PDD allows the infringing undertakings that compensated more than their share to recover a contribution from the other infringing undertakings. The amount of the contribution will be determined in light of each undertaking's relative responsibility for the harm caused by the infringement of competition law. How will the "relative responsibility" of each infringing undertaking be determined?

Answer:

181. Recital 37 PDD explains that a co-infringer should have the right to obtain a contribution from other co-infringers if it has paid compensation amounting to more than its share. The share of each undertaking will be determined as the relative responsibility of a given undertaking in the harm caused by the infringement.

---

[93] Explanatory memorandum in the Proposal for a Directive of the European Parliament and of the Council on certain rules governing actions for damages under national law for infringements of the competition law provisions of the Member States and of the European Union, COM(2013) 404, 11.06.2013, 17.

[94] A. Howard, "Too little, too late? The European Commission's Legislative Proposals on Anti-Trust Damages Actions", *Journal of European Competition Law & Practice* 2013, 458.

[95] Explanatory memorandum in the Proposal for a Directive of the European Parliament and of the Council on certain rules governing actions for damages under national law for infringements of the competition law provisions of the Member States and of the European Union, COM(2013) 404, 11.06.2013, 17.

182. Recital 37 PDD clarifies that the applicable rules of national law should be applied in order to determine the relative responsibility of each infringing undertaking. The same recital refers to turnover, market share and the role in the cartel as examples of relevant criteria for determining the relative responsibility of the infringing undertakings. The relevant national rules are not harmonised by the PDD and have not been harmonised elsewhere in EU law. The only limitation imposed by the PDD in respect of the issue of relative responsibility is that the applicable rules of national law should respect the principles of effectiveness and equivalence (see above, paras 80–87) (recital 37 PDD).

Question:

183. Immunity recipients seem to enjoy wider protection from claims for contribution by other infringing undertakings. What is the scope of this protection for immunity recipients?

Answer:

184. An immunity recipient enjoys special protection as to its contribution in relation to the harm caused by the infringing undertakings. Article 11(5) PDD provides that the amount of contribution by an immunity recipient "shall not exceed the amount of harm it caused to its own direct or indirect purchasers or providers". Hence, even if the immunity recipient played a significant role in the cartel and, on that basis, its relative responsibility for the harm can be judged to be high, its contribution will remain limited to the harm caused to its own direct or indirect purchasers or providers.

185. There is however one exception to the limitation of the immunity recipient's contribution. When the infringement of competition law caused harm to injured parties *other than* the direct or indirect purchasers or providers of the infringing undertakings, the immunity recipient will also have to contribute in the light of its relative responsibility for that harm (Article 11(6) PDD). The reference "injured parties other than the direct or indirect purchasers or providers of the infringers" in Article 11(6) PDD alludes implicitly to injury as a result of umbrella pricing. In the case of umbrella pricing, there are injured parties that have not purchased from the infringing undertakings but that have nevertheless suffered harm as a result of the infringement of competition law. This will be the case, for example, where their suppliers, although not participating in the infringement of competition law, have applied higher prices than they would otherwise have done in the absence of the infringement of competition law.

CHAPTER IV
THE PASSING-ON OF OVERCHARGES

1. GENERAL CONTEXT

186. **Chapter IV PDD** sets out the rules on the passing-on of overcharges. The relevant provisions are contained in Articles 12–16 PDD.

187. "Overcharge" is defined as "the difference between the price actually paid and the price that would otherwise have prevailed in the absence of an infringement of competition law" (Article 2(20) PDD).

188. The right to full compensation implies that the passing-on of overcharges can play a prominent role in claims for damages based on an infringement of competition law.

189. The passing-on of overcharges can be invoked by the defendant (defensive tool or shield) in an action for damages where the defendant can show that the claimant, as the direct purchaser,[96] has passed on the whole or part of the overcharge resulting from the infringement of competition law to the next level(s) in the supply chain. The defendant may try to claim that the direct purchaser did not suffer any harm as he managed to recoup the overcharge by passing it on.[97]

190. The passing-on of overcharges can also be used as an offensive tool against the defendant by an indirect purchaser[98] based on the assertion that the overcharge was passed-on to him by a direct purchaser.

---

96 A direct purchaser is defined as "a natural or legal person who acquired, directly from an infringer, products or services that were the object of an infringement of competition law" (Article 2(23) PDD).

97 T. De Meese, "Private Enforcement" in F. Wijckmans and F. Tuytschaever (eds.), *Horizontal Agreements and Cartels in EU Competition Law*, Oxford, Oxford University Press, 2015, 353, para 8.105.

98 An indirect purchaser is defined as "a natural or legal person who acquired, not directly from an infringer, but from a direct purchaser or a subsequent purchaser, products or services that were the object of an infringement of competition law, or products or services containing them or derived therefrom" (Article 2(24) PDD).

191. Passing-on arguments present a challenge as they create procedural complexity and fragmentation of the damages.[99] The PDD obliges Member States to fully appreciate the "passing-on defence" invoked in the context of claims for damages and has codified the relevant Court judgments.[100]

192. **Recitals 39–44 PDD** provide further details on the passing-on of overcharges.

2. DISCUSSION OF RELEVANT PROVISIONS OF THE PDD

A. ARTICLE 12 PDD: PASSING-ON OF OVERCHARGES AND THE RIGHT TO FULL COMPENSATION

1. To ensure the full effectiveness of the right to full compensation as laid down in Article 3, Member States shall ensure that, in accordance with the rules laid down in this Chapter, compensation of harm can be claimed by anyone who suffered it, irrespective of whether they are direct or indirect purchasers from an infringer, and that compensation of harm exceeding that caused by the infringement of competition law to the claimant, as well as the absence of liability of the infringer, are avoided.

2. In order to avoid overcompensation, Member States shall lay down procedural rules appropriate to ensure that compensation for actual loss at any level of the supply chain does not exceed the overcharge harm suffered at that level.

3. This Chapter shall be without prejudice to the right of an injured party to claim and obtain compensation for loss of profits due to a full or partial passing-on of the overcharge.

4. Member States shall ensure that the rules laid down in this Chapter apply accordingly where the infringement of competition law relates to a supply to the infringer.

5. Member States shall ensure that the national courts have the power to estimate, in accordance with national procedures, the share of any overcharge that was passed on.

---

99 T. De Meese, "Private Enforcement" in F. Wijckmans and F. Tuytschaever (eds.), *Horizontal Agreements and Cartels in EU Competition Law*, Oxford, Oxford University Press, 2015, 353, para 8.106.

100 C.H. Bovis and C.M. Clarke, "Private Enforcement of EU Competition Law", *Liverpool Law Review* 2015, 64.

Question:

193. Article 12(5) PDD states that Member States shall ensure that the national courts have the power to estimate the share of any overcharge that was passed on "in accordance with national procedures". What is meant by the reference to national procedures? What is the interplay between Article 12(5) PDD and Article 12(2) PDD which states that in order to avoid overcompensation Member States shall lay down "procedural rules" appropriate to ensure that compensation for actual loss at any level of the supply chain does not exceed the overcharge harm suffered at that level?

Answer:

194. Article 12 PDD is intended as an "*entrée en matière*". Article 12 PDD brings together all the principles concerning the passing-on of overcharges and summarises what is set out in further detail in Articles 13–15 PDD.

195. The intention was not to regulate *how* the national courts are to estimate the share of any overcharge. The intention was merely to establish the power for national courts to estimate that share. It is left to national law *how* the share of any overcharge is to be estimated so that paragraph 5 does not lay down any substantive rule, but rather a procedural requirement ("in accordance with national procedures"). The point is that national courts must be empowered to estimate the harm and have the necessary national procedures available so as to be able to do so.

196. As to the consistency between Article 12(5) PDD and Article 12(2) PDD, it is not the case that the reference to "procedural rules" in Article 12(2) PDD and the lack of reference to procedural rules but merely to "national procedures" in Article 12(5) PDD implies that the latter is intended as a substantive rule.

197. Reference in this regard can be made to Article 17(1) PDD on the quantification of harm. Article 17(1) PDD also refers to "national procedures" to estimate the amount of the harm if it is established that a claimant suffered harm, but where it is practically impossible or excessively difficult precisely to quantify the harm suffered on the basis of the available evidence. Similar to Article 12(5) PDD, the actual quantification of harm in this context is also left to "national procedures".

198. In order to have a more complete picture, reference must also be made to Article 16 PDD. Article 16 PDD clarifies that the Commission shall issue guidelines for national courts on how to estimate the share of the overcharge passed on to the indirect purchaser. Such guidelines will relate to "the share of the overcharge" and will therefore contain substantive guidance. While the actual procedure is left to national law, the Commission will provide guidance for national courts on the substantive assessment to be made in the context of such estimation. These guidelines will be non-binding. Recital 42 PDD specifies that such guidelines must be clear, simple and comprehensive.

Question:

199. What situation is envisaged in Article 12(3) PDD?

Answer:

200. By means of Article 12(3) PDD, the PDD acknowledges that an injured party who has (fully or partially) passed on the overcharge may still be confronted with harm. Such harm can take the form of a loss of profit due to the fact that the increase of the price has caused a reduction in demand. Hence, the situation envisaged in Article 12(3) PDD is that of a reduced volume of sales due to a price increase resulting from the overcharging by the infringer (see recital 40 PDD). Article 12(3) PDD provides that the injured party has the right to claim and obtain compensation for loss of profit because of a full or partial passing-on of the overcharge.

Question:

201. What situation is envisaged in Article 12(4) PDD?

Answer:

202. Article 12(4) PDD provides that the Member States shall ensure that the rules laid down in Chapter IV PDD on the passing-on of overcharges shall apply accordingly where the infringement of competition law relates to a supply to the infringer.[101] This covers the situation of infringements of competition law concerning supplies to the infringer (e.g. in the case of buyer cartels). Recital 43 PDD explains that, in such cases, the actual loss could result from a lower price paid by infringers to their suppliers.

[101] Recital 43 PDD states: "This Directive and in particular the rules on passing-on should apply accordingly to those cases".

B. ARTICLE 13 PDD: PASSING-ON DEFENCE

> *Member States shall ensure that the defendant in an action for damages can invoke as a defence against a claim for damages the fact that the claimant passed on the whole or part of the overcharge resulting from the infringement of competition law. The burden of proving that the overcharge was passed on shall be on the defendant, who may reasonably require disclosure from the claimant or from third parties.*

Question:

203. Article 13 PDD states that, where passing-on is applied as a defence mechanism, the defendant carries the burden of proving that the overcharge was passed on. At the same time, it is also stated that the defendant can reasonably require disclosure from the claimant or third parties. How will this work in practice, as the information which the defendant would need in order to show that the overcharge was passed on will be very specific (i.e. transaction prices)? Such information will typically be confidential business information.

Answer:

204. It was considered appropriate and necessary for the PDD to provide explicitly that the defendant (i.e. the infringer) carries the burden of proof when passing-on is invoked as a defence. This is in line with the decision practice of the German Supreme Court (the *Bundesgerichtshof*). In other jurisdictions, for example in France, it is not so clear who bears the burden of proof. In order to avoid divergence between the Member States on this point, the PDD contains a clear rule.

205. As a result, the burden of proof is placed on someone who in fact does not hold the necessary evidence. There was therefore a need to provide the possibility of granting access to the relevant information. Reference in this regard can be made to Article 5 PDD on the disclosure of evidence. Article 5 PDD provides that "Member States shall ensure that national courts are able, upon request of the defendant, to order the claimant or a third party to disclose relevant evidence".

206. At the same time, where the claimant or a third party is ordered to disclose such relevant evidence, care must be taken that confidential information is adequately protected. This implies that the confidential nature of the information which is needed to assess a passing-on defence will not as such be a sufficient reason for refusing access. It will be for the national court to impose appropriate measures to ensure that the release of the information is set up in such a manner that the confidentiality of the information is safeguarded while still enabling the infringer to discharge its burden of proof. Article 8(1)(c) PDD provides that Member States shall ensure that national courts are able effectively to impose penalties on parties, third parties and their legal representatives in the event of their failure or refusal to comply with the obligations imposed by a national court order protecting confidential information.

207. A request from the defendant to obtain access to relevant evidence will need to be specific. Article 5(2) PDD states that the evidence must be circumscribed as "precisely" and as "narrowly" as possible. Pursuant to Article 5(3) PDD, it will be up to the national court to judge whether the request is proportionate.

208. As is the case with any disclosure request, it will depend on the willingness of the court whether and to what extent access is granted. The powers of the court are far reaching. For instance, it may be that a third party is ordered to provide access to relevant (and possibly sensitive) evidence in a case in which the third party is not involved. Any party receiving an order to provide access to relevant evidence (including such third parties) cannot apply limits to the disclosure order or refuse to provide access.

209. The aim of Article 5 PDD combined with Article 13 PDD is in fact to ensure that the national court has all the elements available to handle the case within the limits of proportionality, while guaranteeing appropriate protection of any confidential information that may be involved. This implies that the national court has responsibility both for assessing the reasonableness of the request to have access to relevant evidence and for the protection of confidential information.

C. ARTICLE 14 PDD: INDIRECT PURCHASERS

> *1. Member States shall ensure that, where in an action for damages the existence of a claim for damages or the amount of compensation to be awarded depends on whether, or to what degree, an overcharge was passed on to the claimant, taking into account the commercial practice that price increases are passed on down the supply chain, the burden of proving the existence and scope of such a passing-on shall rest with the claimant, who may reasonably require disclosure from the defendant or from third parties.*

2. In the situation referred to in paragraph 1, the indirect purchaser shall be deemed to have proven that a passing-on to that indirect purchaser occurred where that indirect purchaser has shown that:
(a) the defendant has committed an infringement of competition law;
(b) the infringement of competition law has resulted in an overcharge for the direct purchaser of the defendant; and
(c) the indirect purchaser has purchased the goods or services that were the object of the infringement of competition law, or has purchased goods or services derived from or containing them.

This paragraph shall not apply where the defendant can demonstrate credibly to the satisfaction of the court that the overcharge was not, or was not entirely, passed on to the indirect purchaser.

Question:

210. Article 14 PDD deals with the situation where, in an action for damages, the existence of a claim for damages or the amount of compensation to be awarded depends on whether, or to what degree, an overcharge was passed on to an indirect purchaser. The burden of proving the "existence and scope" of the passing-on rests with the indirect purchaser lodging the claim for compensation (Article 14(1) PDD). Article 14(2) PDD determines that the indirect purchaser shall be deemed to have proven the passing-on if points (a)–(c) have been shown. In the event that the indirect purchaser has done so, what is it exactly that has been demonstrated?

Answer:

211. To the extent that each of the points listed in Article 14(2)(a)–(c) PDD has been shown, a rebuttable presumption enters into play that the indirect purchaser has *prima facie* shown the *existence* of a passing-on of an overcharge to him. This also follows from the language in recital 41 PDD ("the latter is regarded as having proven that an overcharge paid by that direct purchaser has been passed on to its level").

212. The *scope* of such overcharge is *not* covered by the presumption. As regards the quantification of the passing-on (i.e. the scope), national courts must have the power to estimate what share of the overcharge has been passed on to the level of the indirect purchasers (recital 41 PDD).

213. The PDD lists three cumulative conditions that must be met before the rebuttable presumption kicks in (Article 14(2)(a)–(c) PDD):

(a) the indirect purchaser has shown that the defendant has committed an infringement of competition law;
(b) the infringement has resulted in an overcharge for the direct purchaser of the infringer; and
(c) the indirect purchaser has purchased the goods or services that were the object of the infringement or has purchased goods or services derived from or containing them.

214. The first condition can be met if, for instance, a cartel decision from a competition authority has been taken. However, this is not a requirement.

215. In accordance with the second condition, the indirect purchaser must show that the infringement of competition law has resulted in "an" overcharge for the direct purchaser of the defendant. If the infringement of competition law consists of a *cartel infringement*, the indirect purchaser can rely on the rebuttable presumption of Article 17(2) PDD which states that it shall be presumed that cartel infringements cause harm. Read in conjunction with recital 47 PDD, which states that "it is appropriate to presume that cartel infringements result in harm, in particular via an effect on prices", the reference to "harm" in Article 17(2) PDD can include harm taking the form of an overcharge.

216. Finally, the indirect purchaser must show that the goods or services it purchased were the object of the infringement of competition law or that it has purchased goods or services derived from or containing them. This implies that the indirect purchaser will need to show *in concreto* (and not in abstract terms) that the goods or services were the object of the infringement or were derived from such goods or services or contains such goods. Recital 41 PDD confirms this reading when referring to an overcharge paid by "that" direct purchaser that has been passed on to "its level". The indirect purchaser will need to reconstruct the link up to the infringer of competition law. This can be a complex exercise when the indirect purchaser is, for instance, fourth or fifth in the supply chain. The third condition for the application of the rebuttable presumption can therefore be fairly complex in certain cases.

217. Article 14(2) PDD clarifies that paragraph 2 shall *not* apply where the defendant (i.e. the infringer) can demonstrate credibly to the satisfaction of the court that the overcharge was not, or was not entirely, passed on to the indirect purchaser. This reflects the rebuttability of the presumption.

D. ARTICLE 15 PDD: ACTIONS FOR DAMAGES BY CLAIMANTS FROM DIFFERENT LEVELS IN THE SUPPLY CHAIN

1. To avoid that actions for damages by claimants from different levels in the supply chain lead to a multiple liability or to an absence of liability of the infringer, Member States shall ensure that in assessing whether the burden of proof resulting from the application of Articles 13 and 14 is satisfied, national courts seized of an action for damages are able, by means available under Union or national law, to take due account of any of the following:
(a) actions for damages that are related to the same infringement of competition law, but that are brought by claimants from other levels in the supply chain;
(b) judgments resulting from actions for damages as referred to in point (a);
(c) relevant information in the public domain resulting from the public enforcement of competition law.

2. This Article shall be without prejudice to the rights and obligations of national courts under Article 30 of Regulation (EU) No 1215/2012.

Question:

218. What is meant by actions for damages "related to the same infringement of competition law"?

Answer:

219. Article 15 PDD relates to actions for damages by claimants from different levels in the supply chain in a passing-on context. The "same infringement of competition law" refers to the fact that the infringement on which the various damages claims of both direct purchasers and indirect purchasers rely is the same. A straightforward example is that where the direct and indirect purchasers rely on the same infringement of competition law that is recorded in the same infringement decision.

Question:

220. What does "to take due account" mean in practice?

Answer:

221. Where actions for damages are introduced by claimants from different levels of the supply chain, national courts seized of such actions must be able to "take due account" of any of the following (Article 15(1)(a)–(c) PDD):

- "related" actions for damages brought by claimants from other levels in the supply chain;
- judgments resulting from such related actions;
- relevant information in the public domain resulting from the public enforcement of competition law.

222. The latter is a broad category and could, for instance, include a press release from the relevant competition authority on a competition law infringement. The addition of "in the public domain" indicates that the court does not actively have to search for such information.

223. The language of "to take due account" was carefully chosen to respect the stipulations of Regulation 1215/2012 on related actions. At the same time, "take due account" also implies that, even if this point is not raised by an involved party, national courts are still able to take into account a related action for damages brought by claimants from other levels in the supply chain.

224. Article 15 PDD aims to offer a solution for the situation where direct and indirect purchasers bring related actions for damages against a defendant in different Member States. This may lead to multiple liabilities for the defendant (the infringer thereby risking to pay damages to the direct purchaser and the indirect purchaser following actions in different Member States which in total may amount to more than full compensation) or, conversely, the absence of liability of the defendant (lack of full compensation).

225. At present, there is no legal instrument that offers a pan-European joinder of actions. Recital 44 PDD states that national courts should have at their disposal appropriate procedural means, such as a "joinder of claims", to ensure that compensation for actual loss paid at any level of the supply chain does not exceed the overcharge harm caused at that level. Recital 44 PDD adds that such means should also be available in cross-border cases. However, at present, there is no EU legal instrument that offers a pan-European joinder of actions.

Question:

226. Article 15 PDD is without prejudice to the rights and obligations of national courts under Article 30 Brussels I bis Regulation. What does this imply?

Answer:

227. It is possible for actions pending before the courts of different Member States to be considered as related (*lis pendens*) within the meaning of Article 30 Brussels I bis Regulation. Under that provision, national courts other than that first seized may stay proceedings or, under certain circumstances, may decline jurisdiction. For the purposes of Article 30 Brussels I bis Regulation, actions are deemed to be related where they are so closely connected that it is expedient to hear and determine them together to avoid the risk of irreconcilable judgments resulting from separate proceedings.

E. ARTICLE 16 PDD: GUIDELINES FOR NATIONAL COURTS

> *The Commission shall issue guidelines for national courts on how to estimate the share of the overcharge which was passed on to the indirect purchaser.*

Question:

228. Will these guidelines be binding for the national courts?

Answer:

229. No, these guidelines will be non-binding.

Question:

230. Is it the intention of the Commission to provide guidelines only on how to estimate the share of the overcharge passed on to the indirect purchaser?

Answer:

231. Although Article 16 PDD refers to the situation of estimating the share of the overcharge which was passed on to the indirect purchaser, the Commission intends to issue guidelines on passing-on in general. In accordance with recital 42 PDD, such guidelines will be clear, simple and comprehensive.

CHAPTER V
QUANTIFICATION OF HARM

1. GENERAL CONTEXT

232. **Chapter V PDD** contains a single provision (Article 17 PDD) and sets out a number of basic principles relating to the quantification of harm.

233. Quantification of harm essentially boils down to assessing how the market in question would have evolved had there been no infringement (recital 46 PDD). This implies a comparison of the actual position of the claimants with the position they would have been in if the infringement had never occurred (counterfactual). This assessment is often a costly and difficult exercise as it usually requires the application of complex economic models.

234. An important starting point is that the PDD acknowledges that the quantification of harm by definition amounts to a hypothetical exercise. On account of this, the PDD proceeds on the assumption (and therefore accepts) that, as a general rule, the damages can never be assessed with complete accuracy (recital 46 PDD).

235. The quantification of harm is not governed by harmonised legal rules. Antitrust harm is to be quantified on the basis of national rules and procedures. The Commission has, however, adopted a Quantifying Harm Communication[102] with the aim of helping national courts and parties to deal with quantification issues. The Communication is accompanied by a Quantifying Harm Practical Guide[103] which offers insights into the types of harm normally caused by anti-competitive practices and provides an overview of the main methods and techniques for calculating the damages due in respect of competition law infringements.[104]

---

102 Communication from the Commission on quantifying harm in actions for damages based on breaches of Article 101 or 102 of the Treaty on the Functioning of the European Union [2013] OJ C167/19.

103 Practical Guide quantifying harm in actions for damages based on breaches of Article 101 or 102 of the Treaty on the Functioning of the European Union, SWD(2013) 205, 11.06.2013.

104 T. De Meese, "Private Enforcement" in F. Wijckmans and F. Tuytschaever (eds.), *Horizontal Agreements and Cartels in EU Competition Law*, Oxford, Oxford University Press,

236. **Recitals 46–47 PDD** provide more context on the PDD principles governing the quantification of harm.

2. DISCUSSION OF RELEVANT PROVISIONS OF THE PDD

A. ARTICLE 17 PDD: QUANTIFICATION OF HARM

> *1. Member States shall ensure that neither the burden nor the standard of proof required for the quantification of harm renders the exercise of the right to damages practically impossible or excessively difficult. Member States shall ensure that the national courts are empowered, in accordance with national procedures, to estimate the amount of harm if it is established that a claimant suffered harm but it is practically impossible or excessively difficult precisely to quantify the harm suffered on the basis of the evidence available.*
>
> *2. It shall be presumed that cartel infringements cause harm. The infringer shall have the right to rebut that presumption.*
>
> *3. Member States shall ensure that, in proceedings relating to an action for damages, a national competition authority may, upon request of a national court, assist that national court with respect to the determination of the quantum of damages where that national competition authority considers such assistance to be appropriate.*

Question:

237. Article 17(1) PDD states that Member States shall ensure that the national courts have the power to estimate the amount of harm in the event that it is practically impossible or excessively difficult "precisely" to quantify the harm suffered on the basis of the evidence available. What is the significance of the word "precisely" in this provision? Does it have any practical implications?

Answer:

238. Quantification of harm implies a comparison with a situation which is by definition hypothetical and can thus never be made with complete accuracy. Recital 46 PDD indicates that, in this context, it is appropriate for national courts to have the power to estimate the amount of the harm caused. This

2015, 355, paras 8.116–8.124.

means that a claim will not fail simply because the harm cannot be quantified in an exact manner. Article 17(1) PDD must therefore be read against the general policy objective of the PDD that injured parties should be able to have the harm compensated and should not be hampered by a practically insurmountable standard or burden of proof.

239. However, in order for national courts to be able to decide that the harm can be estimated instead of being quantified, it should be "practically impossible or excessively difficult precisely to quantify" the harm suffered on the basis of the available evidence. The inclusion of the word "precisely" in this provision has important implications with respect to the burden of proof. It implies that the claimant does not have to render the difficult proof that it is practically impossible or excessively difficult to quantify the harm. The claimant must prove only that the harm cannot be quantified in a precise manner. The inclusion of the word "precisely" could therefore be understood as easing the burden of proof and thus facilitates the switch from a real quantification of harm to an estimation of the harm suffered.

Question:

240. Article 17(2) PDD establishes a rebuttable presumption in favour of the claimant implying that cartel infringements cause harm. What is the practical value of this presumption? Does it have any implications in the context of the passing-on defence as set out in Article 14(2) PDD?

Answer:

241. Recital 47 PDD states that the presumption was created in order to remedy the information asymmetry and some of the difficulties associated with quantifying harm in competition law cases. The presumption does not apply to all competition law infringements covered by the PDD, but only to cartels.[105]

242. Because of the presumption, it will not be possible for judges to decide that a cartel has not caused harm, unless the defendant has proven otherwise. Cartels are presumed to cause harm so that the claimant can focus on the level (quantum) of the damage and not on its existence. If the infringer believes that the cartel has not caused any harm, it will be for the infringer to rebut the presumption. The burden of proof will rest with the infringer.

243. The presumption has significant value in the context of the passing-on discussion. In the event that an indirect purchaser claims damages from the

---

105 For the definition of a cartel, see Article 2(14) PDD.

defendant based on the assertion that the overcharge was passed on to him, the burden of proof of the existence and scope of such a passing-on shall rest with him (Article 14(1) PDD). However, the indirect purchaser shall be deemed to have proven the existence of the passing-on when the conditions set out in Article 14(2) PDD are fulfilled. In the event of a cartel infringement, the second condition (requiring that the infringement should have resulted in an overcharge for the direct purchaser of the defendant) will be met rather easily based on the presumption included in Article 17(2) PDD that cartel infringements result in harm. While this does not affect the burden of proving the scope of the passing on, the presumption can be relied upon by the indirect purchaser to establish the existence of an overcharge.

Question:

244. Article 17(3) PDD grants NCAs the power to assist the national court, if so requested, with respect to the determination of the quantum of damages. In what sense would the NCA be able to assist national courts on quantification issues?

Answer:

245. In practice, such assistance appears to be limited to exceptional cases. In administrative competition law proceedings, the NCA will normally not focus on gathering information that may be directly relevant to the establishment of the quantum of the damages. This is particularly the case in object infringements (such as cartels). In the case of effects-based infringements, the focus will also more likely be on the impact on competition rather than the quantified impact on customers, or the individual customers. Only in exceptional cases will the NCAs be able to offer, if so requested, meaningful assistance on the quantification issue. Relevant information will more likely come from the parties themselves.

CHAPTER VI
CONSENSUAL DISPUTE RESOLUTION

1. GENERAL CONTEXT

246. **Chapter VI PDD** includes Articles 18 and 19 PDD and establishes rules regarding consensual dispute resolution. The measures introduced in this chapter are aimed at encouraging parties to reach a consensual resolution of damages claims. This type of resolution is considered favourably by the PDD as it can often achieve compensation faster and at a lower cost.

247. "Consensual dispute resolution" is defined in Article 2(21) PDD as "any mechanism enabling parties to reach the out-of-court resolution of a dispute concerning a claim for damages".

248. According to Article 2(22) PDD, an agreement reached through such mechanisms is referred to as a "consensual settlement".

249. The principles governing consensual dispute resolution are further clarified by **recitals 48–52 PDD**.

2. DISCUSSION OF RELEVANT PROVISIONS OF THE PDD

A. ARTICLE 18 PDD: SUSPENSIVE AND OTHER EFFECTS OF CONSENSUAL DISPUTE RESOLUTION

> *1. Member States shall ensure that the limitation period for bringing an action for damages is suspended for the duration of any consensual dispute resolution process. The suspension of the limitation period shall apply only with regard to those parties that are or that were involved or represented in the consensual dispute resolution.*

> *2. Without prejudice to provisions of national law in matters of arbitration, Member States shall ensure that national courts seized of an action for damages may suspend their proceedings for up to two years where the parties thereto are involved in consensual dispute resolution concerning the claim covered by that action for damages.*
>
> *3. A competition authority may consider compensation paid as a result of a consensual settlement and prior to its decision imposing a fine to be a mitigating factor.*

Question:

250. Article 18 PDD addresses the (suspensive and other) effects of "consensual dispute resolution". What is the scope of this notion?

Answer:

251. Article 2(21) PDD defines consensual dispute resolution as *any* mechanism enabling parties to reach the out-of-court resolution of a dispute concerning a claim for damages. Recital 48 PDD mentions out-of-court settlements, arbitration, mediation and conciliation as examples of such mechanisms. The notion of "consensual dispute resolution" is to be understood broadly and is thus not limited to consensual or to formal mechanisms. Consensual dispute resolution, for example, also covers negotiations between the parties or their lawyers. It should however be emphasised that, in the case of such informal negotiations, evidence should be provided to prove that the negotiations actually took place in order for the suspensive effects referred to in Article 18 PDD to apply.

Question:

252. Article 18(3) PDD foresees the possibility for competition authorities to consider compensation paid as a result of a consensual settlement reached prior to a fining decision to be a mitigating factor. Does this provision imply that it is forbidden for a competition authority to consider as a mitigating factor compensation following a decision imposing a fine?

Answer:

253. Article 18(3) PDD does not explicitly prohibit this. This could be understood to imply that a competition authority could be allowed to adjust the fines imposed in a decision that has already been adopted following compensation paid as a result of a consensual settlement. At the same time,

Article 18 PDD is created as an incentive for expediting consensual settlements and this incentive will be most effective in the event that the consensual settlement is reached before the fine has been calculated and imposed.

B. ARTICLE 19 PDD: EFFECT OF CONSENSUAL SETTLEMENTS ON SUBSEQUENT ACTIONS FOR DAMAGES

1. Member States shall ensure that, following a consensual settlement, the claim of the settling injured party is reduced by the settling co-infringer's share of the harm that the infringement of competition law inflicted upon the injured party.

2. Any remaining claim of the settling injured party shall be exercised only against non-settling co-infringers. Non-settling co-infringers shall not be permitted to recover contribution for the remaining claim from the settling co-infringer.

3. By way of derogation from paragraph 2, Member States shall ensure that where the non-settling co-infringers cannot pay the damages that correspond to the remaining claim of the settling injured party, the settling injured party may exercise the remaining claim against the settling co-infringer.

The derogation referred to in the first subparagraph may be expressly excluded under the terms of the consensual settlement.

4. When determining the amount of contribution that a co-infringer may recover from any other co-infringer in accordance with their relative responsibility for the harm caused by the infringement of competition law, national courts shall take due account of any damages paid pursuant to a prior consensual settlement involving the relevant co-infringer.

Question:

254. Article 19 PDD discusses the potential effects of consensual settlements on subsequent actions for damages. It is one of the more complex provisions of the PDD. How do the four scenarios covered by this provision work in practice?

Answer:

255. Article 19(1) PDD stipulates that, following a consensual settlement, the claim of the settling injured party should be reduced by the settling infringer's share of the harm caused to it, regardless of whether the amount

of the settlement equals or is different from the relative share of the harm that the settling co-infringer inflicted upon the settling injured party (recital 51 PDD). For example: settling infringer A's share of the harm is 15 out of a total harm of 100 suffered by the injured party. However, infringer A settles with the injured party for 10. In this case, the amount of the settlement differs from the actual level of the damage and hence is lower than the relative share of the harm. In accordance with Article 19(1) PDD, the claim of the injured party will be reduced with settling infringer A's relative share of the harm (which is 15) instead of the amount of the settlement. Hence, the remaining harm for which the injured party can claim against the other parties is reduced to 85 following the settlement (and not 90). Recital 51 PDD clarifies that, without such a reduction, non-settling infringers would be unduly affected by settlements to which they were not a party.

256. Article 19(2) PDD sets the principle that "any remaining claim of the settling injured party shall be exercised only against non-settling co-infringers". Furthermore, as indicated by Article 19(2) PDD, "non-settling co-infringers shall not be permitted to recover contribution for the remaining claim from the settling co-infringer". This provision was inspired by the aim to encourage consensual settlements. If a settling infringer were to continue to be fully jointly and severally liable for the harm caused, even after a consensual settlement was reached, it would be placed in a worse position compared to its co-infringers than it would otherwise be without the consensual settlement (recital 51 PDD). In the context of the aforesaid example this implies that the injured party can claim for the remaining harm of 85 against the other infringers and not against infringer A and, if the other infringers are required to compensate all or part of the harm of 85, they cannot turn to infringer A to seek its contribution to such payment.

257. Article 19(3) PDD provides for a mandatory derogation from the principle foreseen in Article 19(2) PDD. In order to ensure the right to full compensation, the settling injured party is granted the right to exercise the remaining claim against the settling co-infringer where the non-settling co-infringers cannot pay the damages that correspond to such remaining claim. Such remaining claim consists of the claim of the settling injured party reduced by the settling co-infringer's share of the harm, as set out in Article 19(1) PDD (recital 51 PDD). It should however be noted that the latter possibility of claiming damages from the settling co-infringer can be expressly excluded under the terms of the consensual settlement (Article 19(3), subparagraph 2 PDD). Turning again to the concrete example referred to above, national law should enable the injured party to turn towards infringer A in case the other infringers are unable to pay all or part of the harm amounting to 85. In the settlement agreement, infringer A and the injured party can however agree to exclude this possibility.

258. Article 19(4) PDD must be distinguished from the other provisions included in Article 19 PDD. Such other provisions all deal with the claims of *one and the same settling injured party*. Article 19(4) PDD deals with the situation in which settling co-infringers are asked to contribute to damages paid by non-settling co-infringers to *non-settling injured parties*. More specifically, it addresses the situation where a non-settling injured party claims damages from a non-settling co-infringer before a national court and the non-settling co-infringer seeks to recover contribution from a co-infringer who already paid damages to another injured party pursuant to a consensual settlement. In this regard, Article 19(4) PDD states that "[w]hen determining the amount of contribution that a co-infringer may recover from any other co-infringer in accordance with their relative responsibility for the harm caused by the infringement of competition law, national courts shall take due account of any damages paid pursuant to a prior consensual settlement involving the relevant co-infringer". The goal of this provision is to avoid a situation in which settling co-infringers, by paying contribution to non-settling co-infringers, pay a total amount of compensation exceeding their relative responsibility for the harm caused by the infringement (recital 52 PDD).

CHAPTER VII
FINAL PROVISIONS

A. ARTICLE 20 PDD: REVIEW

1. The Commission shall review this Directive and shall submit a report thereon to the European Parliament and the Council by 27 December 2020.

2. The report referred to in paragraph 1 shall, inter alia, include information on all of the following:
(a) the possible impact of financial constraints flowing from the payment of fines imposed by a competition authority for an infringement of competition law on the possibility for injured parties to obtain full compensation for the harm caused by that infringement of competition law;
(b) the extent to which claimants for damages caused by an infringement of competition law established in an infringement decision adopted by a competition authority of a Member State are able to prove before the national court of another Member State that such an infringement of competition law has occurred;
(c) the extent to which compensation for actual loss exceeds the overcharge harm caused by the infringement of competition law or suffered at any level of the supply chain.

3. If appropriate, the report referred to in paragraph 1 shall be accompanied by a legislative proposal.

B. ARTICLE 21 PDD: TRANSPOSITION

1. Member States shall bring into force the laws, regulations and administrative provisions necessary to comply with this Directive by 27 December 2016. They shall forthwith communicate to the Commission the text thereof. When Member States adopt those measures, they shall contain a reference to this Directive or be accompanied by such a reference on the occasion of their official publication. Member States shall determine how such reference is to be made.

2. Member States shall communicate to the Commission the text of the main provisions of national law which they adopt in the field covered by this Directive.

C. ARTICLE 22 PDD: TEMPORAL APPLICATION

1. Member States shall ensure that the national measures adopted pursuant to Article 21 in order to comply with substantive provisions of this Directive do not apply retroactively.

2. Member States shall ensure that any national measures adopted pursuant to Article 21, other than those referred to in paragraph 1, do not apply to actions for damages of which a national court was seized prior to 26 December 2014.

D. ARTICLE 23 PDD: ENTRY INTO FORCE

This Directive shall enter into force on the twentieth day following that of its publication in the Official Journal of the European Union.

E. ARTICLE 24 PDD: ADDRESSEES

This Directive is addressed to the Member States.

ANNEX 1

PRIVATE DAMAGES DIRECTIVE

5.12.2014 EN Official Journal of the European Union L 349/1

I

(Legislative acts)

DIRECTIVES

DIRECTIVE 2014/104/EU OF THE EUROPEAN PARLIAMENT AND OF THE COUNCIL

of 26 November 2014

on certain rules governing actions for damages under national law for infringements of the competition law provisions of the Member States and of the European Union

(Text with EEA relevance)

THE EUROPEAN PARLIAMENT AND THE COUNCIL OF THE EUROPEAN UNION,

Having regard to the Treaty on the Functioning of the European Union, and in particular Articles 103 and 114 thereof,

Having regard to the proposal from the European Commission,

After transmission of the draft legislative act to the national parliaments,

Having regard to the opinion of the European Economic and Social Committee [1],

Acting in accordance with the ordinary legislative procedure [2],

Whereas:

(1) Articles 101 and 102 of the Treaty on the Functioning of the European Union (TFEU) are a matter of public policy and should be applied effectively throughout the Union in order to ensure that competition in the internal market is not distorted.

(2) The public enforcement of Articles 101 and 102 TFEU is carried out by the Commission using the powers provided by Council Regulation (EC) No 1/2003 [3]. Upon the entry into force of the Treaty of Lisbon on 1 December 2009, Articles 81 and 82 of the Treaty establishing the European Community became Articles 101 and 102 TFEU, and they remain identical in substance. Public enforcement is also carried out by national competition authorities, which may take the decisions listed in Article 5 of Regulation (EC) No 1/2003. In accordance with that Regulation, Member States should be able to designate administrative as well as judicial authorities to apply Articles 101 and 102 TFEU as public enforcers and to carry out the various functions conferred upon competition authorities by that Regulation.

(3) Articles 101 and 102 TFEU produce direct effects in relations between individuals and create, for the individuals concerned, rights and obligations which national courts must enforce. National courts thus have an equally essential part to play in applying the competition rules (private enforcement). When ruling on disputes between private individuals, they protect subjective rights under Union law, for example by awarding damages to the victims of infringements. The full effectiveness of Articles 101 and 102 TFEU, and in particular the practical effect of the prohibitions laid down therein, requires that anyone — be they an individual, including consumers

[1] OJ C 67, 6.3.2014, p. 83.
[2] Position of the European Parliament of 17 April 2014 (not yet published in the Official Journal) and decision of the Council of 10 November 2014.
[3] Council Regulation (EC) No 1/2003 of 16 December 2002 on the implementation of the rules of competition laid down in Articles 81 and 82 of the Treaty (OJ L 1, 4.1.2003, p. 1).

and undertakings, or a public authority — can claim compensation before national courts for the harm caused to them by an infringement of those provisions. The right to compensation in Union law applies equally to infringements of Articles 101 and 102 TFEU by public undertakings and by undertakings entrusted with special or exclusive rights by Member States within the meaning of Article 106 TFEU.

(4) The right in Union law to compensation for harm resulting from infringements of Union and national competition law requires each Member State to have procedural rules ensuring the effective exercise of that right. The need for effective procedural remedies also follows from the right to effective judicial protection as laid down in the second subparagraph of Article 19(1) of the Treaty on European Union (TEU) and in the first paragraph of Article 47 of the Charter of Fundamental Rights of the European Union. Member States should ensure effective legal protection in the fields covered by Union law.

(5) Actions for damages are only one element of an effective system of private enforcement of infringements of competition law and are complemented by alternative avenues of redress, such as consensual dispute resolution and public enforcement decisions that give parties an incentive to provide compensation.

(6) To ensure effective private enforcement actions under civil law and effective public enforcement by competition authorities, both tools are required to interact to ensure maximum effectiveness of the competition rules. It is necessary to regulate the coordination of those two forms of enforcement in a coherent manner, for instance in relation to the arrangements for access to documents held by competition authorities. Such coordination at Union level will also avoid the divergence of applicable rules, which could jeopardise the proper functioning of the internal market.

(7) In accordance with Article 26(2) TFEU, the internal market comprises an area without internal frontiers in which the free movement of goods, persons, services and capital is ensured. There are marked differences between the rules in the Member States governing actions for damages for infringements of Union or national competition law. Those differences lead to uncertainty concerning the conditions under which injured parties can exercise the right to compensation they derive from the TFEU and affect the substantive effectiveness of such right. As injured parties often choose their Member State of establishment as the forum in which to claim damages, the discrepancies between the national rules lead to an uneven playing field as regards actions for damages and may thus affect competition on the markets on which those injured parties, as well as the infringing undertakings, operate.

(8) Undertakings established and operating in various Member States are subject to differing procedural rules that significantly affect the extent to which they can be held liable for infringements of competition law. This uneven enforcement of the right to compensation in Union law may result not only in a competitive advantage for some undertakings which have infringed Article 101 or 102 TFEU but also in a disincentive to the exercise of the rights of establishment and provision of goods or services in those Member States where the right to compensation is enforced more effectively. As the differences in the liability regimes applicable in the Member States may negatively affect both competition and the proper functioning of the internal market, it is appropriate to base this Directive on the dual legal bases of Articles 103 and 114 TFEU.

(9) It is necessary, bearing in mind that large-scale infringements of competition law often have a cross-border element, to ensure a more level playing field for undertakings operating in the internal market and to improve the conditions for consumers to exercise the rights that they derive from the internal market. It is appropriate to increase legal certainty and to reduce the differences between the Member States as to the national rules governing actions for damages for infringements of both Union competition law and national competition law where that is applied in parallel with Union competition law. An approximation of those rules will help to prevent the increase of differences between the Member States' rules governing actions for damages in competition cases.

(10) Article 3(1) of Regulation (EC) No 1/2003 provides that '[w]here the competition authorities of the Member States or national courts apply national competition law to agreements, decisions by associations of undertakings or concerted practices within the meaning of Article [101(1) TFEU] which may affect trade between Member States within the meaning of that provision, they shall also apply Article [101 TFEU] to such agreements, decisions or concerted practices. Where the competition authorities of the Member States or national courts apply national competition law to any abuse prohibited by Article [102 TFEU], they shall also apply Article [102 TFEU].' In the interests of the proper functioning of the internal market and with a view to greater legal certainty and a more level playing field for undertakings and consumers, it is appropriate that the scope of this Directive extend to actions for damages based on the infringement of national competition law where it is applied pursuant to Article 3(1) of Regulation (EC) No 1/2003. Applying differing rules on civil liability in respect of infringements of Article 101 or 102 TFEU and in respect of infringements of rules of national competition law which must be applied in the same cases in parallel to Union competition law would otherwise adversely affect the position of

claimants in the same case and the scope of their claims, and would constitute an obstacle to the proper functioning of the internal market. This Directive should not affect actions for damages in respect of infringements of national competition law which do not affect trade between Member States within the meaning of Article 101 or 102 TFEU.

(11) In the absence of Union law, actions for damages are governed by the national rules and procedures of the Member States. According to the case-law of the Court of Justice of the European Union (Court of Justice), any person can claim compensation for harm suffered where there is a causal relationship between that harm and an infringement of competition law. All national rules governing the exercise of the right to compensation for harm resulting from an infringement of Article 101 or 102 TFEU, including those concerning aspects not dealt with in this Directive such as the notion of causal relationship between the infringement and the harm, must observe the principles of effectiveness and equivalence. This means that they should not be formulated or applied in a way that makes it excessively difficult or practically impossible to exercise the right to compensation guaranteed by the TFEU or less favourably than those applicable to similar domestic actions. Where Member States provide other conditions for compensation under national law, such as imputability, adequacy or culpability, they should be able to maintain such conditions in so far as they comply with the case-law of the Court of Justice, the principles of effectiveness and equivalence, and this Directive.

(12) This Directive reaffirms the *acquis communautaire* on the right to compensation for harm caused by infringements of Union competition law, particularly regarding standing and the definition of damage, as stated in the case-law of the Court of Justice, and does not pre-empt any further development thereof. Anyone who has suffered harm caused by such an infringement can claim compensation for actual loss (*damnum emergens*), for gain of which that person has been deprived (loss of profit or *lucrum cessans*), plus interest, irrespective of whether those categories are established separately or in combination in national law. The payment of interest is an essential component of compensation to make good the damage sustained by taking into account the effluxion of time and should be due from the time when the harm occurred until the time when compensation is paid, without prejudice to the qualification of such interest as compensatory or default interest under national law and to whether effluxion of time is taken into account as a separate category (interest) or as a constituent part of actual loss or loss of profit. It is incumbent on the Member States to lay down the rules to be applied for that purpose.

(13) The right to compensation is recognised for any natural or legal person — consumers, undertakings and public authorities alike — irrespective of the existence of a direct contractual relationship with the infringing undertaking, and regardless of whether or not there has been a prior finding of an infringement by a competition authority. This Directive should not require Member States to introduce collective redress mechanisms for the enforcement of Articles 101 and 102 TFEU. Without prejudice to compensation for loss of opportunity, full compensation under this Directive should not lead to overcompensation, whether by means of punitive, multiple or other damages.

(14) Actions for damages for infringements of Union or national competition law typically require a complex factual and economic analysis. The evidence necessary to prove a claim for damages is often held exclusively by the opposing party or by third parties, and is not sufficiently known by, or accessible to, the claimant. In such circumstances, strict legal requirements for claimants to assert in detail all the facts of their case at the beginning of an action and to proffer precisely specified items of supporting evidence can unduly impede the effective exercise of the right to compensation guaranteed by the TFEU.

(15) Evidence is an important element for bringing actions for damages for infringement of Union or national competition law. However, as competition law litigation is characterised by an information asymmetry, it is appropriate to ensure that claimants are afforded the right to obtain the disclosure of evidence relevant to their claim, without it being necessary for them to specify individual items of evidence. In order to ensure equality of arms, those means should also be available to defendants in actions for damages, so that they can request the disclosure of evidence by those claimants. National courts should also be able to order that evidence be disclosed by third parties, including public authorities. Where a national court wishes to order disclosure of evidence by the Commission, the principle in Article 4(3) TEU of sincere cooperation between the Union and the Member States and Article 15(1) of Regulation (EC) No 1/2003 as regards requests for information apply. Where national courts order public authorities to disclose evidence, the principles of legal and administrative cooperation under Union or national law apply.

(16) National courts should be able, under their strict control, especially as regards the necessity and proportionality of disclosure measures, to order the disclosure of specified items of evidence or categories of evidence upon request of a party. It follows from the requirement of proportionality that disclosure can be ordered only where a claimant has made a plausible assertion, on the basis of facts which are reasonably available to that claimant, that the claimant has suffered harm that was caused by the defendant. Where a request for disclosure aims to obtain a category of evidence, that category should be identified by reference to common features of its constitutive elements such as the nature, object or content of the documents the disclosure of which is requested, the time during which they were drawn up, or other criteria, provided that the evidence falling within the category is relevant within the meaning of this Directive. Such categories should be defined as precisely and narrowly as possible on the basis of reasonably available facts.

(17) Where a court in one Member State requests a competent court in another Member State to take evidence or requests that evidence be taken directly in another Member State, the provisions of Council Regulation (EC) No 1206/2001 [1] apply.

(18) While relevant evidence containing business secrets or otherwise confidential information should, in principle, be available in actions for damages, such confidential information needs to be protected appropriately. National courts should therefore have at their disposal a range of measures to protect such confidential information from being disclosed during the proceedings. Those measures could include the possibility of redacting sensitive passages in documents, conducting hearings in camera, restricting the persons allowed to see the evidence, and instructing experts to produce summaries of the information in an aggregated or otherwise non-confidential form. Measures protecting business secrets and other confidential information should, nevertheless, not impede the exercise of the right to compensation.

(19) This Directive affects neither the possibility under the laws of the Member States to appeal disclosure orders, nor the conditions for bringing such appeals.

(20) Regulation (EC) No 1049/2001 of the European Parliament and of the Council [2] governs public access to European Parliament, Council and Commission documents, and is designed to confer on the public as wide a right of access as possible to documents of those institutions. That right is nonetheless subject to certain limits based on reasons of public or private interest. It follows that the system of exceptions laid down in Article 4 of that Regulation is based on a balancing of the opposing interests in a given situation, namely, the interests which would be favoured by the disclosure of the documents in question and those which would be jeopardised by such disclosure. This Directive should be without prejudice to such rules and practices under Regulation (EC) No 1049/2001.

(21) The effectiveness and consistency of the application of Articles 101 and 102 TFEU by the Commission and the national competition authorities require a common approach across the Union on the disclosure of evidence that is included in the file of a competition authority. Disclosure of evidence should not unduly detract from the effectiveness of the enforcement of competition law by a competition authority. This Directive does not cover the disclosure of internal documents of, or correspondence between, competition authorities.

(22) In order to ensure the effective protection of the right to compensation, it is not necessary that every document relating to proceedings under Article 101 or 102 TFEU be disclosed to a claimant merely on the grounds of the claimant's intended action for damages since it is highly unlikely that the action for damages will need to be based on all the evidence in the file relating to those proceedings.

(23) The requirement of proportionality should be carefully assessed when disclosure risks unravelling the investigation strategy of a competition authority by revealing which documents are part of the file or risks having a negative effect on the way in which undertakings cooperate with the competition authorities. Particular attention should be paid to preventing 'fishing expeditions', i.e. non-specific or overly broad searches for information that is unlikely to be of relevance for the parties to the proceedings. Disclosure requests should therefore not be deemed to be proportionate where they refer to the generic disclosure of documents in the file of a competition authority relating to a certain case, or the generic disclosure of documents submitted by a party in the context of a particular case. Such wide disclosure requests would not be compatible with the requesting party's duty to specify the items of evidence or the categories of evidence as precisely and narrowly as possible.

[1] Council Regulation (EC) No 1206/2001 of 28 May 2001 on cooperation between the courts of the Member States in the taking of evidence in civil or commercial matters (OJ L 174, 27.6.2001, p. 1).
[2] Regulation (EC) No 1049/2001 of the European Parliament and of the Council of 30 May 2001 regarding public access to European Parliament, Council and Commission documents (OJ L 145, 31.5.2001, p. 43).

(24) This Directive does not affect the right of courts to consider, under Union or national law, the interests of the effective public enforcement of competition law when ordering the disclosure of any type of evidence with the exception of leniency statements and settlement submissions.

(25) An exemption should apply in respect of any disclosure that, if granted, would unduly interfere with an ongoing investigation by a competition authority concerning an infringement of Union or national competition law. Information that was prepared by a competition authority in the course of its proceedings for the enforcement of Union or national competition law and sent to the parties to those proceedings (such as a 'Statement of Objections') or prepared by a party thereto (such as replies to requests for information of the competition authority or witness statements) should therefore be disclosable in actions for damages only after the competition authority has closed its proceedings, for instance by adopting a decision under Article 5 or under Chapter III of Regulation (EC) No 1/2003, with the exception of decisions on interim measures.

(26) Leniency programmes and settlement procedures are important tools for the public enforcement of Union competition law as they contribute to the detection and efficient prosecution of, and the imposition of penalties for, the most serious infringements of competition law. Furthermore, as many decisions of competition authorities in cartel cases are based on a leniency application, and damages actions in cartel cases generally follow on from those decisions, leniency programmes are also important for the effectiveness of actions for damages in cartel cases. Undertakings might be deterred from cooperating with competition authorities under leniency programmes and settlement procedures if self-incriminating statements such as leniency statements and settlement submissions, which are produced for the sole purpose of cooperating with the competition authorities, were to be disclosed. Such disclosure would pose a risk of exposing cooperating undertakings or their managing staff to civil or criminal liability under conditions worse than those of co-infringers not cooperating with the competition authorities. To ensure undertakings' continued willingness to approach competition authorities voluntarily with leniency statements or settlement submissions, such documents should be exempted from the disclosure of evidence. That exemption should also apply to verbatim quotations from leniency statements or settlement submissions included in other documents. Those limitations on the disclosure of evidence should not prevent competition authorities from publishing their decisions in accordance with the applicable Union or national law. In order to ensure that that exemption does not unduly interfere with injured parties' rights to compensation, it should be limited to those voluntary and self-incriminating leniency statements and settlement submissions.

(27) The rules in this Directive on the disclosure of documents other than leniency statements and settlement submissions ensure that injured parties retain sufficient alternative means by which to obtain access to the relevant evidence that they need in order to prepare their actions for damages. National courts should themselves be able, upon request by a claimant, to access documents in respect of which the exemption is invoked in order to verify whether the contents thereof fall outside the definitions of leniency statements and settlement submissions laid down in this Directive. Any content falling outside those definitions should be disclosable under the relevant conditions.

(28) National courts should be able, at any time, to order, in the context of an action for damages, the disclosure of evidence that exists independently of the proceedings of a competition authority ('pre-existing information').

(29) The disclosure of evidence should be ordered from a competition authority only when that evidence cannot reasonably be obtained from another party or from a third party.

(30) Pursuant to Article 15(3) of Regulation (EC) No 1/2003, competition authorities, acting upon their own initiative, can submit written observations to national courts on issues relating to the application of Article 101 or 102 TFEU. In order to preserve the contribution made by public enforcement to the application of those Articles, competition authorities should likewise be able, acting upon their own initiative, to submit their observations to a national court for the purpose of assessing the proportionality of a disclosure of evidence included in the authorities' files, in light of the impact that such disclosure would have on the effectiveness of the public enforcement of competition law. Member States should be able to set up a system whereby a competition authority is informed of requests for disclosure of information when the person requesting disclosure or the person from whom disclosure is sought is involved in that competition authority's investigation into the alleged infringement, without prejudice to national law providing for *ex parte* proceedings.

(31) Any natural or legal person that obtains evidence through access to the file of a competition authority should be able to use that evidence for the purposes of an action for damages to which it is a party. Such use should also be allowed on the part of any natural or legal person that succeeded in its rights and obligations, including through the acquisition of its claim. Where the evidence was obtained by a legal person forming part of a corporate group constituting one undertaking for the application of Articles 101 and 102 TFEU, other legal persons belonging to the same undertaking should also be able to use that evidence.

(32) However, the use of evidence obtained through access to the file of a competition authority should not unduly detract from the effective enforcement of competition law by a competition authority. In order to ensure that the limitations on disclosure laid down in this Directive are not undermined, the use of evidence of the types referred to in recitals 24 and 25 which is obtained solely through access to the file of a competition authority should be limited under the same circumstances. The limitation should take the form of inadmissibility in actions for damages or the form of any other protection under applicable national rules capable of ensuring the full effect of the limits on the disclosure of those types of evidence. Moreover, evidence obtained from a competition authority should not become an object of trade. The possibility of using evidence that was obtained solely through access to the file of a competition authority should therefore be limited to the natural or legal person that was originally granted access and to its legal successors. That limitation to avoid trading of evidence does not, however, prevent a national court from ordering the disclosure of that evidence under the conditions provided for in this Directive.

(33) The fact that a claim for damages is initiated, or that an investigation by a competition authority is started, entails a risk that persons concerned may destroy or hide evidence that would be useful in substantiating an injured party's claim for damages. To prevent the destruction of relevant evidence and to ensure that court orders as to disclosure are complied with, national courts should be able to impose sufficiently deterrent penalties. In so far as parties to the proceedings are concerned, the risk of adverse inferences being drawn in the proceedings for damages can be a particularly effective penalty, and can help avoid delays. Penalties should also be available for non-compliance with obligations to protect confidential information and for the abusive use of information obtained through disclosure. Similarly, penalties should be available if information obtained through access to the file of a competition authority is used abusively in actions for damages.

(34) Ensuring the effective and consistent application of Articles 101 and 102 TFEU by the Commission and the national competition authorities necessitates a common approach across the Union on the effect of national competition authorities' final infringement decisions on subsequent actions for damages. Such decisions are adopted only after the Commission has been informed of the decision envisaged or, in the absence thereof, of any other document indicating the proposed course of action pursuant to Article 11(4) of Regulation (EC) No 1/2003, and if the Commission has not relieved the national competition authority of its competence by initiating proceedings pursuant to Article 11(6) of that Regulation. The Commission should ensure the consistent application of Union competition law by providing, bilaterally and within the framework of the European Competition Network, guidance to the national competition authorities. To enhance legal certainty, to avoid inconsistency in the application of Articles 101 and 102 TFEU, to increase the effectiveness and procedural efficiency of actions for damages and to foster the functioning of the internal market for undertakings and consumers, the finding of an infringement of Article 101 or 102 TFEU in a final decision by a national competition authority or a review court should not be relitigated in subsequent actions for damages. Therefore, such a finding should be deemed to be irrefutably established in actions for damages brought in the Member State of the national competition authority or review court relating to that infringement. The effect of the finding should, however, cover only the nature of the infringement and its material, personal, temporal and territorial scope as determined by the competition authority or review court in the exercise of its jurisdiction. Where a decision has found that provisions of national competition law are infringed in cases where Union and national competition law are applied in the same case and in parallel, that infringement should also be deemed to be irrefutably established.

(35) Where an action for damages is brought in a Member State other than the Member State of a national competition authority or a review court that found the infringement of Article 101 or 102 TFEU to which the action relates, it should be possible to present that finding in a final decision by the national competition authority or the review court to a national court as at least prima facie evidence of the fact that an infringement of competition law has occurred. The finding can be assessed as appropriate, along with any other evidence adduced by the parties. The effects of decisions by national competition authorities and review courts finding an infringement of the competition rules are without prejudice to the rights and obligations of national courts under Article 267 TFEU.

(36) National rules on the beginning, duration, suspension or interruption of limitation periods should not unduly hamper the bringing of actions for damages. This is particularly important in respect of actions that build upon a finding by a competition authority or a review court of an infringement. To that end, it should be possible to bring an action for damages after proceedings by a competition authority, with a view to enforcing national and Union competition law. The limitation period should not begin to run before the infringement ceases and before a claimant knows, or can reasonably be expected to know, the behaviour constituting the infringement, the fact that the infringement caused the claimant harm and the identity of the infringer. Member States should be able to maintain or introduce absolute limitation periods that are of general application, provided that the duration of such absolute limitation periods does not render practically impossible or excessively difficult the exercise of the right to full compensation.

(37) Where several undertakings infringe the competition rules jointly, as in the case of a cartel, it is appropriate to make provision for those co-infringers to be held jointly and severally liable for the entire harm caused by the infringement. A co-infringer should have the right to obtain a contribution from other co-infringers if it has paid more compensation than its share. The determination of that share as the relative responsibility of a given infringer, and the relevant criteria such as turnover, market share, or role in the cartel, is a matter for the applicable national law, while respecting the principles of effectiveness and equivalence.

(38) Undertakings which cooperate with competition authorities under a leniency programme play a key role in exposing secret cartel infringements and in bringing them to an end, thereby often mitigating the harm which could have been caused had the infringement continued. It is therefore appropriate to make provision for undertakings which have received immunity from fines from a competition authority under a leniency programme to be protected from undue exposure to damages claims, bearing in mind that the decision of the competition authority finding the infringement may become final for the immunity recipient before it becomes final for other undertakings which have not received immunity, thus potentially making the immunity recipient the preferential target of litigation. It is therefore appropriate that the immunity recipient be relieved in principle from joint and several liability for the entire harm and that any contribution it must make vis-à-vis co-infringers not exceed the amount of harm caused to its own direct or indirect purchasers or, in the case of a buying cartel, its direct or indirect providers. To the extent that a cartel has caused harm to those other than the customers or providers of the infringers, the contribution of the immunity recipient should not exceed its relative responsibility for the harm caused by the cartel. That share should be determined in accordance with the same rules used to determine the contributions between infringers. The immunity recipient should remain fully liable to the injured parties other than its direct or indirect purchasers or providers only where they are unable to obtain full compensation from the other infringers.

(39) Harm in the form of actual loss can result from the price difference between what was actually paid and what would otherwise have been paid in the absence of the infringement. When an injured party has reduced its actual loss by passing it on, entirely or in part, to its own purchasers, the loss which has been passed on no longer constitutes harm for which the party that passed it on needs to be compensated. It is therefore in principle appropriate to allow an infringer to invoke the passing-on of actual loss as a defence against a claim for damages. It is appropriate to provide that the infringer, in so far as it invokes the passing-on defence, must prove the existence and extent of pass-on of the overcharge. This burden of proof should not affect the possibility for the infringer to use evidence other than that in its possession, such as evidence already acquired in the proceedings or evidence held by other parties or third parties.

(40) In situations where the passing-on resulted in reduced sales and thus harm in the form of a loss of profit, the right to claim compensation for such loss of profit should remain unaffected.

(41) Depending on the conditions under which undertakings are operating, it may be commercial practice to pass on price increases down the supply chain. Consumers or undertakings to whom actual loss has thus been passed on have suffered harm caused by an infringement of Union or national competition law. While such harm should be compensated for by the infringer, it may be particularly difficult for consumers or undertakings that did not themselves make any purchase from the infringer to prove the extent of that harm. It is therefore appropriate to provide that, where the existence of a claim for damages or the amount of damages to be awarded depends on whether or to what degree an overcharge paid by a direct purchaser from the infringer has been passed on to an indirect purchaser, the latter is regarded as having proven that an overcharge paid by that direct purchaser has

(53) This Directive respects the fundamental rights and observes the principles recognised in the Charter of Fundamental Rights of the European Union.

(54) Since the objectives of this Directive, namely to establish rules concerning actions for damages for infringements of Union competition law in order to ensure the full effect of Articles 101 and 102 TFEU, and the proper functioning of the internal market for undertakings and consumers, cannot be sufficiently achieved by the Member States, but can rather, by reason of the requisite effectiveness and consistency in the application of Articles 101 and 102 TFEU, be better achieved at Union level, the Union may adopt measures, in accordance with the principle of subsidiarity as set out in Article 5 TEU. In accordance with the principle of proportionality, as set out in that Article, this Directive does not go beyond what is necessary in order to achieve those objectives.

(55) In accordance with the Joint Political Declaration of 28 September 2011 of Member States and the Commission on explanatory documents [1], Member States have undertaken to accompany, in justified cases, the notification of their transposition measures with one or more documents explaining the relationship between the components of a directive and the corresponding parts of national transposition instruments. With regard to this Directive, the legislator considers the transmission of such documents to be justified.

(56) It is appropriate to provide rules for the temporal application of this Directive,

HAVE ADOPTED THIS DIRECTIVE:

CHAPTER I

SUBJECT MATTER, SCOPE AND DEFINITIONS

Article 1

Subject matter and scope

1. This Directive sets out certain rules necessary to ensure that anyone who has suffered harm caused by an infringement of competition law by an undertaking or by an association of undertakings can effectively exercise the right to claim full compensation for that harm from that undertaking or association. It sets out rules fostering undistorted competition in the internal market and removing obstacles to its proper functioning, by ensuring equivalent protection throughout the Union for anyone who has suffered such harm.

2. This Directive sets out rules coordinating the enforcement of the competition rules by competition authorities and the enforcement of those rules in damages actions before national courts.

Article 2

Definitions

For the purposes of this Directive, the following definitions apply:

(1) 'infringement of competition law' means an infringement of Article 101 or 102 TFEU, or of national competition law;

(2) 'infringer' means an undertaking or association of undertakings which has committed an infringement of competition law;

(3) 'national competition law' means provisions of national law that predominantly pursue the same objective as Articles 101 and 102 TFEU and that are applied to the same case and in parallel to Union competition law pursuant to Article 3(1) of Regulation (EC) No 1/2003, excluding provisions of national law which impose criminal penalties on natural persons, except to the extent that such criminal penalties are the means whereby competition rules applying to undertakings are enforced;

(4) 'action for damages' means an action under national law by which a claim for damages is brought before a national court by an alleged injured party, or by someone acting on behalf of one or more alleged injured parties where Union or national law provides for that possibility, or by a natural or legal person that succeeded in the right of the alleged injured party, including the person that acquired the claim;

(5) 'claim for damages' means a claim for compensation for harm caused by an infringement of competition law;

(6) 'injured party' means a person that has suffered harm caused by an infringement of competition law;

[1] OJ C 369, 17.12.2011, p. 14.

(7) 'national competition authority' means an authority designated by a Member State pursuant to Article 35 of Regulation (EC) No 1/2003, as being responsible for the application of Articles 101 and 102 TFEU;

(8) 'competition authority' means the Commission or a national competition authority or both, as the context may require;

(9) 'national court' means a court or tribunal of a Member State within the meaning of Article 267 TFEU;

(10) 'review court' means a national court that is empowered by ordinary means of appeal to review decisions of a national competition authority or to review judgments pronouncing on those decisions, irrespective of whether that court itself has the power to find an infringement of competition law;

(11) 'infringement decision' means a decision of a competition authority or review court that finds an infringement of competition law;

(12) 'final infringement decision' means an infringement decision that cannot be, or that can no longer be, appealed by ordinary means;

(13) 'evidence' means all types of means of proof admissible before the national court seized, in particular documents and all other objects containing information, irrespective of the medium on which the information is stored;

(14) 'cartel' means an agreement or concerted practice between two or more competitors aimed at coordinating their competitive behaviour on the market or influencing the relevant parameters of competition through practices such as, but not limited to, the fixing or coordination of purchase or selling prices or other trading conditions, including in relation to intellectual property rights, the allocation of production or sales quotas, the sharing of markets and customers, including bid-rigging, restrictions of imports or exports or anti-competitive actions against other competitors;

(15) 'leniency programme' means a programme concerning the application of Article 101 TFEU or a corresponding provision under national law on the basis of which a participant in a secret cartel, independently of the other undertakings involved in the cartel, cooperates with an investigation of the competition authority, by voluntarily providing presentations regarding that participant's knowledge of, and role in, the cartel in return for which that participant receives, by decision or by a discontinuation of proceedings, immunity from, or a reduction in, fines for its involvement in the cartel;

(16) 'leniency statement' means an oral or written presentation voluntarily provided by, or on behalf of, an undertaking or a natural person to a competition authority or a record thereof, describing the knowledge of that undertaking or natural person of a cartel and describing its role therein, which presentation was drawn up specifically for submission to the competition authority with a view to obtaining immunity or a reduction of fines under a leniency programme, not including pre-existing information;

(17) 'pre-existing information' means evidence that exists irrespective of the proceedings of a competition authority, whether or not such information is in the file of a competition authority;

(18) 'settlement submission' means a voluntary presentation by, or on behalf of, an undertaking to a competition authority describing the undertaking's acknowledgement of, or its renunciation to dispute, its participation in an infringement of competition law and its responsibility for that infringement of competition law, which was drawn up specifically to enable the competition authority to apply a simplified or expedited procedure;

(19) 'immunity recipient' means an undertaking which, or a natural person who, has been granted immunity from fines by a competition authority under a leniency programme;

(20) 'overcharge' means the difference between the price actually paid and the price that would otherwise have prevailed in the absence of an infringement of competition law;

(21) 'consensual dispute resolution' means any mechanism enabling parties to reach the out-of-court resolution of a dispute concerning a claim for damages;

(22) 'consensual settlement' means an agreement reached through consensual dispute resolution.

(23) 'direct purchaser' means a natural or legal person who acquired, directly from an infringer, products or services that were the object of an infringement of competition law;

(24) 'indirect purchaser' means a natural or legal person who acquired, not directly from an infringer, but from a direct purchaser or a subsequent purchaser, products or services that were the object of an infringement of competition law, or products or services containing them or derived therefrom.

9. The disclosure of evidence in the file of a competition authority that does not fall into any of the categories listed in this Article may be ordered in actions for damages at any time, without prejudice to this Article.

10. Member States shall ensure that national courts request the disclosure from a competition authority of evidence included in its file only where no party or third party is reasonably able to provide that evidence.

11. To the extent that a competition authority is willing to state its views on the proportionality of disclosure requests, it may, acting on its own initiative, submit observations to the national court before which a disclosure order is sought.

Article 7

Limits on the use of evidence obtained solely through access to the file of a competition authority

1. Member States shall ensure that evidence in the categories listed in Article 6(6) which is obtained by a natural or legal person solely through access to the file of a competition authority is either deemed to be inadmissible in actions for damages or is otherwise protected under the applicable national rules to ensure the full effect of the limits on the disclosure of evidence set out in Article 6.

2. Member States shall ensure that, until a competition authority has closed its proceedings by adopting a decision or otherwise, evidence in the categories listed in Article 6(5) which is obtained by a natural or legal person solely through access to the file of that competition authority is either deemed to be inadmissible in actions for damages or is otherwise protected under the applicable national rules to ensure the full effect of the limits on the disclosure of evidence set out in Article 6.

3. Member States shall ensure that evidence which is obtained by a natural or legal person solely through access to the file of a competition authority and which does not fall under paragraph 1 or 2, can be used in an action for damages only by that person or by a natural or legal person that succeeded to that person's rights, including a person that acquired that person's claim.

Article 8

Penalties

1. Member States shall ensure that national courts are able effectively to impose penalties on parties, third parties and their legal representatives in the event of any of the following:

(a) their failure or refusal to comply with the disclosure order of any national court;

(b) their destruction of relevant evidence;

(c) their failure or refusal to comply with the obligations imposed by a national court order protecting confidential information;

(d) their breach of the limits on the use of evidence provided for in this Chapter.

2. Member States shall ensure that the penalties that can be imposed by national courts are effective, proportionate and dissuasive. The penalties available to national courts shall include, with regard to the behaviour of a party to proceedings for an action for damages, the possibility to draw adverse inferences, such as presuming the relevant issue to be proven or dismissing claims and defences in whole or in part, and the possibility to order the payment of costs.

CHAPTER III

EFFECT OF NATIONAL DECISIONS, LIMITATION PERIODS, JOINT AND SEVERAL LIABILITY

Article 9

Effect of national decisions

1. Member States shall ensure that an infringement of competition law found by a final decision of a national competition authority or by a review court is deemed to be irrefutably established for the purposes of an action for damages brought before their national courts under Article 101 or 102 TFEU or under national competition law.

2. Member States shall ensure that where a final decision referred to in paragraph 1 is taken in another Member State, that final decision may, in accordance with national law, be presented before their national courts as at least prima facie evidence that an infringement of competition law has occurred and, as appropriate, may be assessed along with any other evidence adduced by the parties.

3. This Article is without prejudice to the rights and obligations of national courts under Article 267 TFEU.

Article 10

Limitation periods

1. Member States shall, in accordance with this Article, lay down rules applicable to limitation periods for bringing actions for damages. Those rules shall determine when the limitation period begins to run, the duration thereof and the circumstances under which it is interrupted or suspended.

2. Limitation periods shall not begin to run before the infringement of competition law has ceased and the claimant knows, or can reasonably be expected to know:

(a) of the behaviour and the fact that it constitutes an infringement of competition law;

(b) of the fact that the infringement of competition law caused harm to it; and

(c) the identity of the infringer.

3. Member States shall ensure that the limitation periods for bringing actions for damages are at least five years.

4. Member States shall ensure that a limitation period is suspended or, depending on national law, interrupted, if a competition authority takes action for the purpose of the investigation or its proceedings in respect of an infringement of competition law to which the action for damages relates. The suspension shall end at the earliest one year after the infringement decision has become final or after the proceedings are otherwise terminated.

Article 11

Joint and several liability

1. Member States shall ensure that undertakings which have infringed competition law through joint behaviour are jointly and severally liable for the harm caused by the infringement of competition law; with the effect that each of those undertakings is bound to compensate for the harm in full, and the injured party has the right to require full compensation from any of them until he has been fully compensated.

2. By way of derogation from paragraph 1, Member States shall ensure that, without prejudice to the right of full compensation as laid down in Article 3, where the infringer is a small or medium-sized enterprise (SME) as defined in Commission Recommendation 2003/361/EC ([1]), the infringer is liable only to its own direct and indirect purchasers where:

(a) its market share in the relevant market was below 5 % at any time during the infringement of competition law; and

(b) the application of the normal rules of joint and several liability would irretrievably jeopardise its economic viability and cause its assets to lose all their value.

3. The derogation laid down in paragraph 2 shall not apply where:

(a) the SME has led the infringement of competition law or has coerced other undertakings to participate therein; or

(b) the SME has previously been found to have infringed competition law.

4. By way of derogation from paragraph 1, Member States shall ensure that an immunity recipient is jointly and severally liable as follows:

(a) to its direct or indirect purchasers or providers; and

(b) to other injured parties only where full compensation cannot be obtained from the other undertakings that were involved in the same infringement of competition law.

Member States shall ensure that any limitation period applicable to cases under this paragraph is reasonable and sufficient to allow injured parties to bring such actions.

([1]) Commission Recommendation 2003/361/EC of 6 May 2003 concerning the definition of micro, small and medium-sized enterprises (OJ L 124, 20.5.2003, p. 36).

3. A competition authority may consider compensation paid as a result of a consensual settlement and prior to its decision imposing a fine to be a mitigating factor.

Article 19

Effect of consensual settlements on subsequent actions for damages

1. Member States shall ensure that, following a consensual settlement, the claim of the settling injured party is reduced by the settling co-infringer's share of the harm that the infringement of competition law inflicted upon the injured party.

2. Any remaining claim of the settling injured party shall be exercised only against non-settling co-infringers. Non-settling co-infringers shall not be permitted to recover contribution for the remaining claim from the settling co-infringer.

3. By way of derogation from paragraph 2, Member States shall ensure that where the non-settling co-infringers cannot pay the damages that correspond to the remaining claim of the settling injured party, the settling injured party may exercise the remaining claim against the settling co-infringer.

The derogation referred to in the first subparagraph may be expressly excluded under the terms of the consensual settlement.

4. When determining the amount of contribution that a co-infringer may recover from any other co-infringer in accordance with their relative responsibility for the harm caused by the infringement of competition law, national courts shall take due account of any damages paid pursuant to a prior consensual settlement involving the relevant co-infringer.

CHAPTER VII

FINAL PROVISIONS

Article 20

Review

1. The Commission shall review this Directive and shall submit a report thereon to the European Parliament and the Council by 27 December 2020.

2. The report referred to in paragraph 1 shall, inter alia, include information on all of the following:

(a) the possible impact of financial constraints flowing from the payment of fines imposed by a competition authority for an infringement of competition law on the possibility for injured parties to obtain full compensation for the harm caused by that infringement of competition law;

(b) the extent to which claimants for damages caused by an infringement of competition law established in an infringement decision adopted by a competition authority of a Member State are able to prove before the national court of another Member State that such an infringement of competition law has occurred;

(c) the extent to which compensation for actual loss exceeds the overcharge harm caused by the infringement of competition law or suffered at any level of the supply chain.

3. If appropriate, the report referred to in paragraph 1 shall be accompanied by a legislative proposal.

Article 21

Transposition

1. Member States shall bring into force the laws, regulations and administrative provisions necessary to comply with this Directive by 27 December 2016. They shall forthwith communicate to the Commission the text thereof.

When Member States adopt those measures, they shall contain a reference to this Directive or be accompanied by such a reference on the occasion of their official publication. Member States shall determine how such reference is to be made.

2. Member States shall communicate to the Commission the text of the main provisions of national law which they adopt in the field covered by this Directive.

Article 22

Temporal application

1. Member States shall ensure that the national measures adopted pursuant to Article 21 in order to comply with substantive provisions of this Directive do not apply retroactively.

2. Member States shall ensure that any national measures adopted pursuant to Article 21, other than those referred to in paragraph 1, do not apply to actions for damages of which a national court was seized prior to 26 December 2014.

Article 23

Entry into force

This Directive shall enter into force on the twentieth day following that of its publication in the *Official Journal of the European Union*.

Article 24

Addressees

This Directive is addressed to the Member States.

Done at Strasbourg, 26 November 2014.

For the European Parliament	*For the Council*
The President	*The President*
M. SCHULZ	S. GOZI

ANNEX 2

LIST OF PARTICIPANTS IN THE CLOSED WORKSHOP

SPEAKERS

Eddy De Smijter
(DG Competition – Head of Unit: ECN and Private Enforcement)

Martin Seegers
(Cartel Damage Claims)

Ben Bornemann
(Cartel Damage Claims)

Anneli Howard
(Monckton Chambers)

PARTICIPANTS

BELGIUM
CONTRAST
EUROPEAN & BUSINESS LAW
Frank Wijckmans
Filip Tuytschaever
Luc Demeyere
Maaike Visser
Sarah Jaques

BULGARIA
Boyanov & co
Peter Petrov

CROATIA
Divjak, Topic & Bahtijarevic
Mario Krka

CYPRUS
Chrysses Demetriades & Co
Polyvios Panayides

DENMARK
Horten
Andreas Christensen
Marie Gøthgen Clasen

FINLAND
Ditmar & Indrenius
Ilkka Leppihalme

GERMANY
Arnecke Sibeth
Werner Blau

Commeo LLP
Stephanie Pautke

GREECE
Kyriakides Georgopoulos Law Firm
Anastasia Dritsa
Violeta Panagiotopoulou
Vasiliki Kriketou

HUNGARY
SBGK
Péter Lukácsi

ITALY
Dandria Studio Legale
Gennaro d'Andria
Francesco Alongi

THE NETHERLANDS
Stek
Jan Erik Janssen

Banning N.V.
Esra van der Wolk
Minos van Joolingen

Maverick Advocaten N.V.
Bas Braeken
Diederik Schrijvershof

POLAND
Hansberry-Tomkiel
Dorothy Hansberry-Bieguńska

Modzelewska & Paśnik
Malgorzata Modzelewska de Raad
Piotr Paśnik

PORTUGAL
SRS Advogados
Gonçalo Anastácio
André Fojo

SPAIN
J&A Garrigues S.L.P
Konstantin Jörgens
José Luis Azofra Parrondo

Pérez-Llorca
Oriol Armengol

INDEX

Reference is made to the paragraph numbers.

www.ingramcontent.com/pod-product-compliance
Ingram Content Group UK Ltd.
Pitfield, Milton Keynes, MK11 3LW, UK
UKHW051923100926
8556IPUK00021B/1336